Shirin Ramzanali Fazel

Far from Mogadishu

Edited and with foreword of Simone Brioni

First published in 1994 by
Datanews Edizioni - Rome

Reprinted in 1997 by
Datanews Edizioni - Rome

2nd Edition published in 1999 by
Datanews Edizioni - Rome

Re-published in 2013 by
Laurana Reloaded - Milan
Bilingual edition

Current Publication

5th Edition published in 2016
Copyright 2016, by Shirin Ramzanali Fazel

Far from Mogadishu

All rights reserved. No part of this publication may be reproduced or transmitted in any form by any means, electronic or mechanical, including photocopying, recording or any information storage or retrieval system, without the prior permission in writing from the Author.

ISBN-13: 978-1717341792

ISBN-10: 1717341799

Published in the UK

*To my husband,
you are the salt and the honey of my life.*

Contents

Rainbow	1

PART ONE

The Fairytale Country	5
Bondere	5
My Neighbourhood	7
The Triumphal Arch	8
The funerals	10
Meetings	11
Afgooye, Outing in the Country	12
The Seasons	13
The Last Bards	15
The Rain	15
Cape Guardafui	16
Young Metropolitans	18
The Tailors	19
Gezira	20
The Flag	21

PART TWO

The Departure	25
Vegia Nuara	26
Loneliness	27
A Cup of Sugar	27
Close Encounters	29
"Stasera mi butto"	30
The First Day of Spring	34
Ramadan	35
Love Dances	36

The Well	37
Far Away Lands	41
Siesta	42

PART THREE

Deep Nostalgia	45
Third World	46
Southern Hemisphere	46
Termini Station	48
The Big Apple	48
The Hotel Porter	50
Zanzibar	51
The Purse	52
Diani Beach – Mombasa	54
Madafu	55

PART FOUR

Somalia	59
The Camel Drivers	60
Sacrilege	61
War Games	62
The New Beirut	63
The Innocent	65
Living in Waiting	67
Pilgrims of the Past	68
The Exiles	68
Hussein	71

PART FIVE

African Heart	75
Cultural Leftover	76
The Pharisees and Mother Teresa	77
Neologisms and Hypocrisies	77
The Suitcase	78
Africa	79

PART SIX

A Special Day	83
Fantastic Destinations	83
Children	85
Silent Warrior Woman	85
The New Poor	86
Do You Like Italy?	87
The Love Piano	88

PART SEVEN

Airports	93
Leila	96
The Wedding	99
The Shop	102
Hamar Adde	107
Eid Al-Adha	110
New Generations	115
My Friend in London	119
Universal TV	120
Text Messages	123

PART EIGHT

The Village	129
DNA	134
Badante	136
The Hijab	140
Far from Mogadishu, 20 Years Later	143
The Rise of a New Dawn	147

'A Dialogue that Knows no Border between Nationality, Race or Culture': *Simon Brioni*	149
References	165
Bibliography	174
My Thanks	181

Far from Mogadishu

*We build walls to defend
ourselves and in the
end we realize
they are prisons
that suppress our
feelings*

Rainbow

We are not entering your towns
with arrogance and armed with guns,
but with respect.
Our colourful and smiling faces
revive your gray and monotonous towns.
We bring you our friendship,
our human values,
our culture with many new dialects,
music, dance and strong, spicy food
like our character.
In exchange we receive your hostile sneers.
But if you treat us as if we come
to dirty your already polluted towns,
if you hated us even before meeting,
or if you pitied us to relieve your conscience,
you have been completely mistaken.

# PART ONE

The Fairytale Country

There was a time when my country was the country of fairytales, a country where every child would want to grow and play.

There was an old toothless storyteller in the square, and young women selling fruits along the streets. Exotic fruits that tasted sweet and pungent, with bright colours stolen from the sun. Soft, hairy lambs bleated loudly as if to take part of the joy around them.

There were immense green fields of corn, where children played hide-and-seek. There were huge mango trees that filled the air with their scent, and nearby a river flowed where children would plunge in, laughing loudly. There were giant turtles and dunes of the finest warm sand where they rolled around. There were stores where the little ones would go to buy sweets that tasted of far away lands.

There were neighbourhoods with narrow alleyways with no names that children knew by heart. There were cats, hens, *dik-dik* and monkeys as pets. There were ageless villages where children ran naked with smiling faces. There were elephants, lions, hippos and many camels that drank noisily from muddy rivers. There was an immense blue sky with great white clouds that never finished telling stories.

Bondere

Bondere is one of the oldest neighbourhoods in Mogadishu. At dawn the call to prayer from the nearby mosque, enters softly from the window we keep open during the night. The sound of dragging feet and water flowing from the tap spreads in the sleeping house. Later it is the sticky aroma of cardamom, cinnamon, cloves and sugar boiling for the morning tea that is swimming in the rooms, while the smell of frying eggs and thin pancakes travels furtively to our neighbours. On Fridays, it is the juicy lamb's liver sizzling with a lot of onions that makes my stomach rumble.

The woman carrying fresh milk and eggs comes to our door daily. When the air starts to become heavy, it's time for the cart of drinking water to stop at our gate. It is pulled by the same short donkey; he turns his head searching for my little hand holding a banana. His happiness lasts a few seconds, and then his eyes are dull again.

A loud hoarse voice is piercing the neighbourhood,

"Bananas, watermelons, *limoni*, onions, garlic, tomatoes, mangos, chilli and *bombelmo*, grapefruit."

It's the man selling fruits and vegetables. His calloused feet are dry like an old leather shoe and are covered with dust. His skull cap is stained with sweat. He is always smiling, or maybe he looks as if he were smiling because of the missing teeth.

A young boy is drumming with a fork on an aluminium tray, selling gummy homemade sweets, followed by the vendor of green mint syrup ice lollies, yelling, "*Gellado*, ice cream."

The garbage man takes a break, eating a pancake and sipping a cup of tea that my mother offered him.

When the sun is at its zenith and even the bees are too lazy to fly, the nomad knocks. He supplies camel milk and butter. He is carrying a big jar carved from wood and holds a long wooden spoon. The last drops fall in the bowl, like pearls. The *ghee* is thick, yellow and smells of cow.

Beggars tap at the gate softly and with their humble voice implore; they receive a few coins or a bowl of spaghetti left from the night before.

The muezzin calls the believers for the second prayer of the day.

After lunch only the sound of the rusted fan wanders in the shadowy rooms. In the afternoons our house is filled with the sound of the radio that mingles with the laughter and gossip of our visiting friends and neighbours.

Again the air is filled with the scent of spiced tea and ginger coffee.

The sun is sinking very fast, the stars are preparing to twinkle, while a melodic voice is calmly calling us to pray *maghrib*, sunset. Soft lights appear in the houses, and the scent of burning frankincense is inviting the angels to protect the neighbourhood.

My Neighbourhood

The doors of the houses of Mogadishu were never closed. There was no privacy, but it was normal. The whole neighbourhood was like a big family. The neighbours would participate in your pain or joy.

If someone was ill, there would be more coming and going than usual; even the beggars would send prayers for the well-being of the sick person. Seldom would a robbery take place and if it happened, the booty consisted of a few pots and pans, a pair of used shoes, or the washing hanging on the rope. This event would become the talk of the day. People would shake their heads, cursing the poor thief, "This is not one of us, a God fearing person. He is not from our neighbourhood."

They would keep on telling and adding stories until a new event took over. The second marriage of an old man to a young girl becomes the juicy gossip, for both sexes. Men normally say, "He has the right to get married; we are allowed to have four wives." Women say, "Poor Halima, her husband married a young one." "We should not trust men, not even when they get old."

The argument becomes controversial when a young girl runs away from home to get married against the will of her parents, "She comes from a good family, what a shame." "The family did not educate her well." "*Eeb*, shame!" "Why did the family not get her a spouse sooner? Girls should get married early." "They can bring shame."

Preparing food, we would never count only our close family members, but we would always add a few extra portions, which were not enough anyway. Friends, extended family and neighbours would come at lunch time without notice and would simply sit at the table. I would go so far as to say that even domesticated cats would go next door and expand their territory to enrich their own menu.

Women invited to marriages would borrow gold bracelets, earrings, sandals from each other. They would prepare homemade biscuits, tattoo their hands with henna, dye their hair, give feet and back massages to each other. When a new baby was born, it was a big event.

Mothers could leave their young ones, knowing that at home, there was always an aunt, an *ayeeyo*, grandmother, who would keep an eye on them.

Every moment was marked with the exchange of voices, laughter, songs, gossip that had been part of our lives since we were babies, so that it would be unthinkable to cut them out.

The Triumphal Arch

My *ayeeyo* is inspecting me like a general would check his soldiers. Her expert eye runs over my cotton pleated frock to see that it is spotless. She adjusts the white ribbons holding my two long plaits, looks down at my white socks to see if they are pulled up to my knees, and if my brown leather shoes with the big buckle are shining. With the blink of an eye, she decides I am ready to be seen by the whole world.

We march out of the house and walk towards the main road, via Roma. The hot afternoon is cooling, and the streets are still busy. We don't have to wait long for an ape-taxi. The popular tricycle is covered by a white canvas, and the driver is wearing flip-flops. We sit at the back and the man is ready to go after hearing the command of *ayeeyo*: "To the Giardini."

I enjoy the breeze and the smell of dust. I have fun watching the people walking the busy roads. We pass a tired donkey carrying water tanks; I can almost touch it. Blaring *Vespas* driven by young men overtake us. The whole vehicle is shaking and turning on the bumpy road. The noise is coming from all around us. The trip takes us a few minutes; we get down and *Nana* counts the silver coins to pay the driver.

She holds my hand and we climb the few steps to the park. There are cement benches under this huge Triumphal Arch built by the Italians in the fascist era. Tall palm trees move with the light wind, and there are lots of purple and white periwinkle flower beds. All around mostly white children with their nannies play quietly. We are not allowed to touch the flowers, but we can run and chase pigeons. Holding dry twigs we disturb green and grey young lizards hiding beneath smooth stones.

I am not happy to come to this park. I can't roll on the floor, sweat or take off my shoes. My dress has to be spick and span, so do my hands. I sit near my *Nana*, bored, my legs dangling from the bench.

She is chatting with other women, inhaling the sea breeze. I throw my head back and look at the sky. It's blue; the clouds are wandering slowly. I wish I were a cloud. I search for the white moon that is not shining. Nimble pigeons feast on worms around the square. Young couples dreaming, holding hands, lost in each other's stare and sit in the shadowy corners. The sound of the traffic is filtered by the leaves of the *neem* trees planted along the road.

Here comes the ice-cream man; we are all waiting for him. I lick and suck the juicy, red, syrup flavoured, ice square. I hold it in my mouth; it melts faster than I thought. I close my eyes; this is the best part of our trip. I am careful not to get even a drop of the red colour on my white dress. The ice numbs my lips, and with my eyes shut I don't feel the little red drop running down my chin and falling on my immaculate collar.

I open my eyes; the sky is still blue, and I can see the leafy palm trees whispering in the air and the white clouds strolling.

The Funerals

Many people attended my Nana's funeral: all our extended family, some travelling from far, our friends and the whole neighbourhood. They wanted to share that tremendous loss.

Since my childhood I had heard my *Nana* say, "One day we are all going to die. Death is inevitable. Allah, have Mercy on us. Let us pray for our dead. To Allah we belong and to Him we shall return."

Living in Italy I have never heard people talking about death. They would say, "He is missing, or she is missing." I could not understand, missing, where did they go? It took me time to understand that they were afraid to say, "He died."

Death is taboo talk in Western societies where people exorcise this last appointment of life confining it to a hospital, or to a nursing home, in the unwitting attempt to keep death away from their homes.

In an Islamic society, death is natural, and the whole family is expected to gather and assist the dying person. The funeral has great importance and the rituals to follow are very important.

The body is washed by members of the family, perfumed and shrouded in white cloth. There is no difference of status between rich and poor. A special funeral prayer takes place in the mosque, and it is the duty of every Muslim to take part in the ceremony. Old and young men accompany the corpse to the cemetery for the burial, and a simple white stone will remind us of her resting place. At home, people prayed and recited the Quran, cooked rice, goat and camel meat. They stayed with us; some spent the night on mattresses and others on the floor, under a ceiling of bright stars.

Today, 1992, in the tragedy that struck Somalia, there is also a lack of water needed to wash the bodies. Our dead are buried in common graves.

Meetings

My mother would not allow me to attend the meetings with her girlfriends. I was forbidden to enter our large sitting room with the blue sofas. So, careful not to be seen, I would peep and eavesdrop behind the door. I would capture fragments of conversations and laughter.

Women would often meet for tea. They would come wearing long, colourful dresses, or hand woven *guuntino*, a traditional Somali women's dress, their head and shoulders covered in transparent silk *garbasaar*. Dangling golden earrings made by the finest artisan in filigree would show off the latest model in vogue. Spiced tea is served: cardamom, cinnamon and cloves. The aroma is strong, the colour dark, almost black, and very sweet.

They chat and laugh for a long time, then my mother puts burning coal in the *dabqaad*, brazier, and adds *uunsi*, myrrh, before offering it to the ladies. Blocks of scented resin, melting slowly, send a swirling, fragrant breeze that they hold under their dresses. Perfumed clouds caress their skin and hide in their petticoats. Then the brazier is raised under their black curly hair, where the unique *oudh*, resin and wood of the tropical Agar (Aquilaria) and Gyrinops trees, fragrance is trapped.

Tiny glass bottles with Arabic writing, full of dense oily perfume served on a silver tray go around, passing from one red-painted hand to another. Gold rings shine from slim, caramel fingers.

The afternoon passes slowly. When the shadows of the trees get longer, they hug and kiss each other, leaving the house quietly.

Afgooye, Outing in the Country

My childhood memories take me back to our trips to the countryside on Fridays. Offices and schools are closed. My mum, my dad, some friends and I would squeeze in our Fiat 1400 and leave the city. The car windows are open and soon the intense smell of the bush fills our lungs. Straight, bumpy roads are surrounded by acacia trees and small, thorny bushes; meek camels are guided by a lonely man wrapped in a white cotton cloth carrying a long cane. He does not move from the road, or turn. He holds his head straight; his hair is groomed in an umbrella-shaped style, as if he were wearing a crown. He raises his long arm like a stick of liquorice to salute.

We are going to Afgooye, a tranquil farmers' village, where a river flows and serves as an oasis for the camels. The surrounding vegetation is lush and the honey-coloured river runs slowly.

The trip always means lunch at "Cristiani", the best one of the two Italian restaurants in Afgooye. The specialities are handmade *pasta al forno* and chicken *alla diavola*. Under massive, leafy mango trees and wild, colourful, purple and pink bougainvillea, the tables are spread with red and white chequered tablecloths. Tall waiters, dressed in long, white impeccable tunics with a large red band holding their waist and a carmine top hat *fez* on their heads that makes them look taller, come to take orders.

While all around us, in different dialects, adults gesticulate, talk loudly, laugh, smoke and drink Chianti wine from green-bellied bottles embellished with straw; we youngsters have fun.

We play, run and chase the cats. Grey, white, ginger, black, tabby cats, some limping, the older ones with scars of tough fights tattooed on their fur, others with rib bones sticking out from the side of their chest. Fluffy, unfriendly kittens with dirty eyes hide under the tables. Cats are everywhere; waiters carrying trays kick them and stamp their feet trying to frighten them, but they are veterans and are not scared of anything.

We venture down the path that leads to the kitchen to spy on the chefs. They are busy, and look angry. A big guy with an apron smeared with blood bangs the chicken with the meat pounder to flatten it, raising his hands in the air, shouting at his helper.

Sweaty men, with red eyes from the smoke, are cooking at the grill. Chunks of red coal burst, sending clouds of chicken fat burning into the air. It is as if a war is going on. In this side of the restaurant, there is not one cat around.

One day the owner brought a big cage. All the children went to see the new attraction: a lion. The new game among the children becomes to fling leftover meat through the steel bars. The old lion with a shaggy mane does not scare us. He is walking nervously in the bare, concrete cage, up and down, on his big paws without getting tired. Jerkily, he shakes his stiff tail in the air like a whip, and he roars sadly.

In the afternoon after lunch my parents take me to the plantations along the Shebelle River to buy pulpy mangos, pink grapefruits, sweet guavas, tiny round shining limes and bunches of bananas. On our way back, I fall asleep, rocked by the movement of the car.

The Seasons

Many times I have been asked by my Italian friends, "How many seasons do you have in Somalia? Does it rain in your country? How nice, it is always summer?"

It must be very difficult for them to understand. Their idea is, either beautiful white sand beaches and fun all the time, or a country with drought, no crops and people dying.

If I thought of the seasons in Italy when I was studying the Italian curriculum in Mogadishu, my ideas were influenced by poems, nursery rhymes, geography, science, novels and the movies we used to watch. A fantasy in my head: soft white flakes falling from the sky... I was living a fairytale. No comparison to when I saw the snow for real.

We have four seasons in Somalia. When I was growing up as a child in the city, they did not affect our life style. The rainy season was fun, and when it was very hot we used to put on the fan. But the climate regulates the life of the nomadic pastoral people, who are the majority of the Somali population.

Jilal goes from December to March and it is the hardest dry season for the nomads and their families. The soil gets arid, it cracks, pasture is scarce and livestock drops dead of thirst. Only the strong camel survives. It is a struggle between nature and men. In many families, people remember the cattle lost in this period, the child who died or the elderly who could not make it through harsh times.

Gù is our spring, it goes from April to June. Nature renews its miracle: the desert turns into green and lush pasture, the bush is flowering. Marriages take place, people meet, social activity abounded. Even the age of a person is determined by how many *Gù* he has lived.

Good times do not last long, so the second dry season, *Xagaa*, from July to September, hits. This time it is not too dramatic. Dust storms, vegetation and pasture become dry. Nomadic families travel in search of the best grazing and water for their animals. Women dismantle their huts, and camels are loaded with household goods. Herds of goats, sheep and cattle are reunited by men. When the group moves, even the children help to look after the little goats. Everything respects a ritual that has gone on for centuries, handed down orally from father to son.

Dayr is the shortest rainy season, it goes from October to late November. Sudden strong showers that do not last long, leave the land filled with puddles. Happy, giggling children enjoy splashing in the water. The scent of the bush gets very intense, but the nomads know it will not last for long, so they settle for a short period. Expert hands prepare *ghee*, and dry meat to be consumed during the terrible *Jilal*.

I have great respect for the nomads. They are free, strong people. In their journeys, they are guided by the stars and the knowledge of their ancestors. Men who communicate with nature and their livestock. Men who respect and love their herds, and who are ready to sacrifice their cattle only in case of extreme necessity. Men and women who preserve the secret of our traditions.

The Last Bards

Somalis have always been a people with rich imagination, gifted with a great eloquence and an innate joy of self-expression.

In the undergrowth, the camel drivers gathered under the acacias, improvised poetry competitions and debates. The winners were compensated with animals and fame.

At weddings, births and funerals, the storytellers were always present. The children were never at a loss for new nursery rhymes and enchanting fables.

Lovers recited verses to their sweethearts. They would tease one another with improvised rhymes. During the dictatorship, songwriters clandestinely used satire like the sole arm against the regime.

The dialects were rich with colourful expressions and abundant proverbs.

Love, fidelity, betrayals, peace and birth: everything transmuted into verses.

The Rain

It was a celebration, when I was a child and rain drops were falling in Mogadishu. I have never seen an umbrella open on a showery day. On the contrary! Umbrellas were used by the elderly on very hot days, to shield them from the unforgivable sun's rays.

If I think back, I can see dark clouds carrying heavy rain and I can hear the unmistakable tick tack of warm raindrops on metal roofs. The scent of damp soil was so strong it left an indelible trace in my olfactory memory. Streets would flood for several days, and leave puddles where we would let our paper boats float.

Even when it was windy and the rain was strong, nobody would run to avoid getting wet. Even the young women, usually chaste, were not so shy as to hide their firm breasts that showed under the soggy *guntino*. Me and my friends, giggling, would push each other under the strong jet of water coming from the gutters. The whole of nature was sharing that immense joy: the rain!

Cape Guardafui

At the time of the Italian empire, ships departed from Italy, full of men in search of adventure. Their destination, the Horn of Africa. The journey is long, the climate hot and sticky, but they are full of enthusiasm. Young men looking forward to explore vast jungles and conquer dark girls with big, wild eyes. Soon after crossing the Suez Canal they see the Egyptian desert. The vessel enters the Red Sea and the air gets torrid.

After a few days, they reach Cape Guardafui, on the extreme tip of the Horn. Men are getting ready for their new life: the labourer becomes an engineer, the bricklayer becomes an architect and the nurse becomes a doctor.

The memory of the victims buried in the village is still alive in the elderly. The little cemetery was named after the white doctor who took care of them.

Professions are changed but not the language. The environment is changed but not the mentality of these men. Time is passing without evolution. Small oases are created to preserve habits of a distance homeland. It is in these microcosms that someone like me, who had never seen Italy, would feel it close.

The streets, schools, churches, barracks, monuments, shops, cinemas, restaurants, bars, hotels had names like: Bar Impero, Bar Nazionale, La Croce del Sud, La Mediterranea, La Pergola, El Trocadero, Tre Fontane, Cappuccetto Nero, Via Roma, Corso Italia, Caserma Podgora, Cinema Centrale, Supercinema, Scuola Regina Elena, Ospedale de Martino, Chiesa del Sacro Cuore. This little Italy that, surrounded me, made my city an Italian provincial town.

In the Mogadishu of my childhood, white is the predominant colour: safari bush jackets, trousers, our school uniforms, hats and the nun's long dresses.

I was brought up in this world. I studied Italian language at school, from the nursery rhymes to the poems of Pascoli. In spite of my knowledge of the Italian language and culture, I could feel the annoying superiority shown by the Italian residents. It was like living in a parallel dimension where two realities would live together without integrating.

Independence brought little change. Radio Mogadishu still broadcast news, songs, and daily programmes from Italy. The national newspaper, "Il Corriere della Somalia", was printed in Italian, as Italian was the country's official language. Milan, Inter and Juventus football teams had their fans, but the oasis created by the Italian empire shrank visibly. La Casa d'Italia remained its last fortress, packed with people nostalgic for the fascist era, always ready to criticise everything and everyone, but always with an excuse not to leave the country.

They did not want to leave Somalia, where time was marked by a human rhythm and houses were spacious, with lush gardens of bougainvillea, oleanders and papaya trees. They did not want to leave houses in which many obliging servants were always present, and stories about safari games full of emotions were told around a fireplace in the savannah, while the boys fixed the tents for bedtime. Those long African nights, draped in mosquito nets, lulled by hyena's laughter and lion's breath, under a full moon; the magic will flow in their veins and possess their minds: it is the *Mal d'Africa*.

Young Metropolitans

The shop in front of the American Embassy was the only one to have the latest records during my teenage years. My girlfriends and I were grooving proudly to the rhythms of James Brown's *Say it loud, I am black and proud*. Wilson Pickett would squeeze every drop of our sweat while dancing *Funky Broadway* and Aretha Franklin's blues blew our minds.

Parties were given to welcome young graduates coming back from Western countries. We would share their new ideas and meld them with our dreams. We shared a common enthusiasm for our sincere ideals. We would learn the latest fashion dance steps from the United States and U.K. The banned book *La Settimana Nera*, by Enrico Emanuelli, was photocopied and circulated in our underground circle.

At the Terzo Mondo bookstore we discovered Léopold Senghor's poems and we gained awareness of our African heritage. It was the only bookstore were it was possible to find essays and publications on the Pan-Africanism, a growing political movement theorized by Kwame Nkrumah.

Afternoons were dedicated to learning English at the British Council and American Embassy. French, German and Russian courses were also available at their cultural centres. Films in original languages were shown, followed by interesting debates. President Gamal Abdel Nasser sent hundreds of teachers to Mogadishu for us to learn Arabic.

The Somali National Theatre was full of people enjoying the biting satire of our changing society. The theatre used to host artists from different countries. My eyes were glued to the stage, watching the costumes and dances of various ethnic groups from the Soviet Union and People's Republic of China.

Somali doctors were graduating from China, and at the hospital acupuncture was the trend. Eating out was fun, we used Chinese chopsticks and we discovered the taste of soy sauce.

The whole world was coming to us, through newspapers, magazines, and protest songs of Bob Dylan and Joan Baez. We had no television in the country, but I had not missed it. Every evening I used to go to the cinema with my dad and enjoy our evenings under the stars. If I think of those days and compare it with current times, I know we were extremely fortunate.

The Tailors

The tailors of my city, Mogadishu, were the most loved. The few professional ones would choose their clientele, and women would kill to have a dress made by one of them. Sometimes they would cut the design according to their own taste and convince the client that it was the best one for her figure.

After shopping in the Tamarind Souk for colourful cotton and silk fabrics, ladies would head with their best friends to the tailor's shop. Aydarous would never disappoint any of us. He knew how to hide large hips, enhance a short neck; he knew how to bring out the beauty of a woman. Very discreetly, his nimble fingers would pin the dress for the finishing touch, and you would walk out feeling like a queen.

His shop was always busy. Piles of textile, zips, buttons, wrinkled tape measure, rulers; the noise of the pedal sewing machines; pieces of cotton thread and tiny waste materials littered the floor. From the ceiling an old fan would turn slowly, pushing the hot air in circles. On the wall, there were faded pages of glamour journals. The long table was used only by the *maestro*, whose expert hands guided sharp scissors in cutting the cloth. Lots of magazines to choose from, some with missing pages. Crumpled old sheets of wedding, evening, summer and winter dresses would tempt and confuse the choice. And then, after a long consultation, the design was altered anyway. The tailor would sketch the new idea on a piece of paper.

Behind the thick curtain a familiar face would be trying a frock in front of a mirror. That mirror had a spell to make you look taller.

A woman with a serious face, accompanied by her four daughters, is waiting to be served. She is holding glittering fabrics; we could guess they will attend a wedding.

Everyday young women, women in menopause, skinny, short, tall, round, pregnant, fair, ebony, crowded the *sartoria*, and left in the air a cloud of blended perfumes. My friends and I would chitchat, laugh and snoop at other customers' dresses. We would beg Aydarous to swear that he would keep our design unique. He would vow, but vainly.

It could happen that the dress was not ready on the promised date; it was useless to get angry. He was overwhelmed by work. So, patiently, we would not move from the shop until he cut the fabric and started sewing. In the meantime, we would sing along to popular songs from the radio, sipping cold Fanta and Coca-Cola. We would laugh at jokes told by his ever-present friend, who was there to impress young girls.

Gezira

Gezira. Our first outing. We are newly-wed and we can be together without being watched by my family. I can still remember, my *ayeeyo*, my grandmother, holding her rosary and pushing the beads, her lips moving, producing no sound, and her cataract eyes vigilant on us; my terrible little cousin, always ready to spy and tell tales on us; my dad reading his newspaper behind thick spectacles and my mum entering the room unexpectedly with her feline gait, like a shadow, to exorcise every temptation.

In Gezira we are alone, with only the infinite ocean, fine white sand and little crabs crawling under the sun. It is like we are the only ones in this world. The waves are calm, the day is warm and we are never tired of looking at each other, and holding each other, floating. We cuddle, you look into my eyes. We hug; you swim and carry me lightly in the water. The sea is immense like our love.

Birmingham, 2012. Many years have passed and this picture comes to my mind, silent tears roll on my cheeks. I wrote:

> Young and innocent, our heart filled with love, we thought the world was in our hands.
>
> Then came the sadness of leaving home.
>
> Travelling, discovering, learning, suffering, cheering and understanding that home is wherever our family lives.
>
> The world is in our hands now that we have the wisdom to love many lands, languages, people and plant seeds of memory everywhere.

The Flag

1st July 1960, Independence Day. Thousands of people come from all over the country. Some travel by bus, others on foot and by camels. It is a big day; they flood the town's main square. The crowd is thrilled and sings patriotic *buraambur*, women's poetry. At midnight, for the first time, the Somali flag is hoisted. It waves in the sky.

The bright blue flag looks like the immense blue sky and, in the middle, there is a five-pointed white star. The points represent the five Somali lands ripped off by colonists: Jibuti under the French, N.F.D., bordering Kenya, under the British government, Ogaden under the Ethiopian, Italian Somalia, and the British Somaliland. Lands that were never reunited.

The big Somali dream will be to unite the territories.

PART TWO

The Departure

The night before my departure I could not sleep. So many feelings ran through my body. I was scared, in a state of anxiety, excited, thrilled, a roller-coaster of emotions. I could not believe the time had come to leave my home. I was not alone; my husband and my two month old baby were with me, this tiny, defenceless creature. We were very young.

It was the first time I was leaving my family, my friends, my country. It had been a very difficult choice, but we had no other option. The military regime was in its second year and things in Mogadishu were deteriorating. People were living in an anguished atmosphere; you were not free to talk anymore. The ruling junta had ears and eyes everywhere.

The airport was crowded. My parents, friends and relatives were there to say goodbye. My daughter was hugged, embraced, blessed. I feared I was not going to have her back. My mum in silent tears, the pain painted on my dad's face, my extended family mumbling, whispering, others saying in loud voices, "Have a safe journey! Allah will protect you! We will pray for you! Take care of the baby! Write to us, let us have your news, do not forget us! You are blessed!"

Some were crying, others waving their arms. So much confusion surrounded, I felt as if I were in a dream.

I was focusing on my destination, a country I knew: Italy. A country I have studied all my life, since nursery school. I had many Italian friends and schoolmates. Most of them had a Somali mother and an Italian father. It was like I had lived in the shadow of Italy for ages. I have studied history, Garibaldi, Mazzini and their struggle for Italian unification. At the cinema, Totò and Sordi were my favourite actors and I appreciated the sensitivity of the film director Pietro Germi. *Pasta al forno, bignè* and *cappuccino* were not exotic foods, but something I used to eat very often. The songs of Modugno, Mina, Gianni Morandi accompanied my adolescence. Dante, Pirandello, Pavese's writings a pillar in my studies. Now I was ready to walk the soil of a country that had shrouded my world since I was born.

The aeroplane was packed with Italian refugees. Young and elderly who had lived almost all their lives in Somalia. Long, sad faces, in their eyes panic, resignation, anger. Many familiar names, Fiat employees, shop and garage owners, Italo-Somali families. There was no happiness fluttering in the belly of this huge plane. I was bewildered.

I remember how my young husband and I held hands tightly during the take-off. Not a word from our lips, only our eyes were speaking, and promising each other all the love, trust, and the strength necessary for a small family leaving its country.

Even today I am touched deeply when I see a new immigrant. It is as if a small wound inside me had never healed.

Vegia Nuara

My arrival in Italy was a disaster. It was late autumn. I had never seen fog before. I only knew the clear blue sky of Mogadishu. The oppressive, leaden Novara, lost in the paddy field was for me an unknown Italy, far from the idea I had in my mind.

When winter comes back I remember our walks at the *Allea* Park, our footsteps crushing piles of yellow, dead leaves. Naked trees, a grey sky, fog and cold in the air. Silence around me, only rushing passers-by, with a quick look, trying to guess who we were and where we came from.

Our little girl sitting in her buggy, with her bright red bonnet, gave me the courage to carry on.

My husband and I, close to one another, trying to keep warm, were walking towards the city centre. Palazzo Bellini, Broletto, Piazza Duomo, il Battistero, la Basilica di San Gaudenzio. We were surrounded by people speaking a new dialect, *Novarese*, a dialect that conquered our hearts.

We had no friends in that city and we were in search of human tenderness.

Loneliness

In the loneliness of that provincial town, aloof and inhospitable, I would ask myself many times, "Where is my home? My peaceful garden, my papaya tree, my blue sky, my friends? My mum, with all her blessings, my father's reassuring presence? The little shop filled with the aroma of coffee beans, cumin, sesame oil, dry henna, dates, coconut sweets and smiling faces, dusty shelves, and persistent flies, where I used to chat and buy groceries? My neighbourhood of white houses, with its noisy children playing in the shadow, tabby cats sleeping, songs from the radio and familiar people where everybody knew my name? Where is my charming neighbour with gazelle's eyes and innocent smile?"

I am standing here, waiting for the bus, around me a gloomy town where nobody knows my name, but only the colour of my skin.

A Cup of Sugar

Arriving in Italy, in a provincial town, I discovered the colour of my skin.

Mogadishu, my home town, situated in the costal Benadir region, kissed by the Indian Ocean, was multi-ethnic. People of different ethnic groups over centuries traded goods, cohabited and mingled peacefully. In the streets and alleys sounds of different dialects, ancient neighbourhoods with their coral stone houses. There lived Arabs, mainly Yemenis, in more recent times Egyptians, Syrians, people from India. Italians, whom I had as schoolmates since my nursery years. A big number of meticci, children born from Italian fathers and Somali mothers. Chinese were mostly doctors in Government hospitals, Soviets were the technocrats and military advisers. American, English, French, German, Canadian's were the diplomats. Because of the large number of foreigners, we were not curious about skin colour and nationality.

Instead, in that small, provincial Novara, we were the only ones to have dark skin. Everybody looked at us. People stopped us just to touch my daughter. It was very annoying, made me feel like a rare creature. People would look, make loud comments, stroke my baby, but not offer their friendship.

I would stay at home, where I felt secure. I would not want to go out alone. I would wait for my husband to come from work to take my daughter out for her daily stroll. With him I was safe.

One afternoon the doorbell rang. It was not the time for my spouse to be back, so, a bit frightened, I looked from the peephole. I saw a woman. I opened the door, a smiling young lady holding a cup spoke, "I am your neighbour, from the other side of the wing, could I borrow some sugar?"

"*Sì, ... sì con molto piacere, entra.*" I was so happy to speak with someone. I invited her in, and made a cup of spiced Somali tea. Vittoria was my first friend in Italy, and I am glad to say that we are still good friends.

Later she confided me that the cup of sugar was just an excuse. We were sharing a partition wall: on her side, there was their sitting room; on my side, my baby's room. She could hear me singing, "*Huuwaya huuwaa, habarta ma joogto, kor iyo koonfur ay jirta...*", a lullaby in Somali.

She was sure we were not Italians, but then she would hear, "*La bella lavanderina che lava i fazzoletti, per i poveretti della città...*", another lullaby, but this time in Italian, without any accent, and she could not make up her mind.

Tired of having her ear glued to the wall, trying to understand who we were, and where we came from, she decided to make the first move.

It is memorable, the evening that Vittoria invited us for dinner, and we got frog's legs on our plates.

Close Encounters

When I first came to Novara it seemed to me that all the Italians were deaf. I would stop and ask a passer-by: "*Per cortesia, mi può indicare via Monte Nero?*", will you please direct me to via Monte Nero?

And the person would look at me and start to articulate words clearly, using verbs in the infinitive tense in a loud voice: "*Camminare diritto, sempre diritto, vedere incrocio, girare destra, trovare via Monte Nero.*"

The same would happen if I were at the fruit market or in a shop. They would repeat the information several times, as if I were deaf. I could not understand what was going on. I thought some of them had not been to school and had problems in using the verbs correctly.

As time passed by and I met more people, I was asked weird questions like, "Did you live in a hut? Did you have roads and cars where you come from? Do you have cows? Did you wear a grass skirt? Are there cannibals in Africa?"

Some people, thinking to give me a compliment, would say, "You are not black; black like the ones we see on television. You are beautiful, you look like us."

I was upset, and only then I understood the ignorance about me. They knew the Africans of the documentary films in black and white, the Africans of Tarzan and *Gone with the wind*, the ones who would roll their big eyes and talk with a lousy accent. I was angry, not with the ordinary people, but with the politicians. In Somalia, we have studied the Italian curriculum; we knew the name of the rivers, mountains, poets, heroes, history, grammar, but Italians knew nothing about us.

Children in Italy had the figure of the Negro with the grass skirt on their school books. He would have a big ring hanging from his nose and a bone between his coarse hair. In some shops, I saw the same figure on a tin left there by the church to collect money; I was ashamed.

In the following years, things did not change. Curiosity towards the foreigner was becoming intolerance. I started getting involved in the community, offering my time to create an intercultural dialogue. We started going to several schools to speak about our culture, and religion. Students would interact with us. Answering them we would dispel the stereotypes created by the mainstream media. I collaborated with a group of Italian volunteers, helping immigrant women get a better understanding of the new laws on immigration. I believe that each one of us can contribute in a positive way to the community and that we can learn from each other.

"*Stasera mi butto*"

Mum suddenly decided to come and visit us, exactly one year after my departure. I wish she had come in summer, and not late autumn. I did not want her to have the shock I felt, caused by the grey, gloomy weather. The cold sneaking arrogantly through layers of thick woollen jumpers, a fake sun that would not deliver any warmth, naked trees, days of drizzling rain, and a crushing sky with no clouds. Even the dogs in the streets looked sad.

Knowing my mother, I could not tell her, "*Hooyo*, mother, it is better for you to come in summer; it's too cold for you now. "She would have taken it like an insult, a way of telling her, "We don't want you to come."

It was our decision to leave the country, in my letters I have never told her how homesick I was. I showed my family the strong, brave, young woman who, alone with her husband and baby daughter, was able to make it far from home.

How could I tell her how depressed I felt, walking the streets of a foreign town, where nobody knew my name, but only the colour of my skin?

How could I tell her I have not spoken for days with an adult except my husband when he was back from work?

How could I tell her I would have gone mad if I had not had my baby girl with me?

How could I tell her I did not know the name of my neighbour?

How could I tell her that tea, in Italy, tastes like camel piss?

Time is passing slowly, and I have to swallow sorrows.

I missed going to the movies under a roof of blinking stars.

I missed raindrops on my face, my noisy squint-eyed neighbour.

I missed the *adhan*, call for prayer, from the little mosque behind my house, the shouting of the vegetable vendor on my street, giggling with my best friend.

I missed the afternoon nap, when the whole town is having a *siesta*.

I missed my pet Titam, the old turtle, that used to pull out her wrinkled neck to eat lettuce from my hand.

I missed my dad's brown, smiling eyes looking at me from behind his glasses.

I missed the touch of my mother's hands on my head, whispering her prayers.

I missed my friends bursting into my home at all times.

I missed the smell of cardamom, ginger and cumin escaping from the cooking pots.

I missed our noisy streets and the shadow of the *neem* trees when the sun got merciless.

I missed the weddings, where cakes never taste the same.

My happiness was now my small family: my daughter's loud smile, her crawling faster than a kitten, the first white teeth cutting her soft, pink gum, her heartbeat next to mine.

I was so happy my mother was coming! I could actually touch her. Her voice trembling from the long distance call, me telling her, "*Hooyo*, please cover properly, the weather is very cold here."

In Mogadishu nobody ever speaks of the weather. Here they have an entire television programme, *Che tempo fa*, presented by the famous *Colonnello Bernacca*. He has a big audience. I found out that, after a lot of explanations of turbulence, isobars, winds and other complications, nothing changes: it is always cold!

My husband had to leave by train to go to Rome to pick up mum. I could not sleep the whole night. The next day, as soon as I heard the key in the lock, I jumped. She was here, my mum in front of my eyes. We hugged. She looked so vulnerable, so fragile in that large, thick, coarse woollen, long, dark green dress. I had no idea where she could have picked a material like that in Mogadishu. Only her colourful red *shaash*, scarf, tied on her head disclosed her strong character.

Clearly, she was tired from the long trip. After dinner and a lot of *sheeko sheeko* about our lives, we all went to bed. Next day it was Saturday and my husband did not have to go to the office. I try not to make any noise going into the kitchen. I am washing the dishes, left in the sink the night before; my hands are immersed in white foam and my heart is singing. I hear a warm voice behind me, "Good morning."

"Good morning *hooyo*, did you sleep well?"

My mum sits, putting her elbows on the table, her lower lip drops and her right eyebrow rises slightly. I know that expression very well. I carry on rinsing the glasses.

Her reply is fast and has nothing to do with my question, "Has the *boyessa* come today to clean the house?"

I turn to her and laugh, saying, "*Hooyo*, here nobody has a maid. At least not common people like us. Only rich people can afford one, and sometimes not for the whole day. I do all the house chores."

She is very serious, her voice that of a woman used to giving orders, "What are you doing in a country where you cannot afford a maid? Wouldn't it be better for you to come back to Mogadishu?"

I do not answer. I knew she was always against us going away. I did not want to start an argument.

"Mum, I will take you out to visit the city, only the two of us, like old times."

She puts up a smile. I had in mind to take her shopping. I could not let her go around with that horrible garment. People would not stop to stare at us. We enter a department store; after a long discussion, I beg her to try a classical trouser and a matching jacket. When she walks out of the changing room, I my jaw drops. She is stunning. Her slender figure with all the curves in the right place, the red colour of the fabric showing up her black skin. She looks so young.

Fantastic! I have decided that she will not have the time to take it off. I rush to pay and we leave the shop, before she can change her mind. *Hooyo* is mad at me; she could have killed me, if the cold air had not made her bite her tongue.

I am not finished with her yet. I have to get rid of the headscarf. A wig shop, just around the corner, comes to my mind. I drag her in there; a bored woman with a big, fake chignon approaches us. We are her only clients. We are surrounded by plastic heads. I feel I am in a cemetery of scalps. A musty smell hits my nose.

I cannot go back, I have a mission to carry out: mum has to turn into a modern woman.

The saleslady knows her job well, she makes mum try every kind of wig: short, straight, curly, long, ringlets, black, dark brown. Sometimes a giggle comes out of us. Mum is tired; she gives up. I convince her to wear a wig otherwise she will get sick if the cold gets in her head. Finally a short, soft, black haired wig looks perfect on her. She is changing her physiognomy, this lady is not my mum, I am thinking.

I can see her expression; she also could not recognise herself.

I don't care; what I want to avoid for her is being looked at by the people of this city. I want her not to feel different from the others. I want her to blend. Not to stand out like a beautiful, exotic bird surrounded by penguins. I love her so much; dressed like this they would not notice her. We walk outside, close to each other. I hold her arm. I fondle her. I want her to forgive me. I notice we still attract the attention of the passers-by. A man with an incredulous look stops and pointing at her says, "Lola Falana… she is Lola Falana!"

My mum still does not know that Lola Falana is the only black singer, and show girl on Italian television.

The First Day of Spring

My second child was born on the first day of spring; all around, nature was at its renewal, flowering, blossoming, chirping birds and delicate butterflies, meadows covered in tiny daisies. At Ospedale San Giuliano, nurses were very kind and, in the labour room, the excitement for this event was palpable: the birth of the first non-white baby in that hospital.

The staff members were disappointed to see a very fair-skinned infant. Samira was really beautiful: she did not have wrinkled skin, the flat nose and red face, like a beetroot, that most newborn have. I was very grateful to Allah for this healthy creature. Cuddling and feeding her was a blessing. I was under her spell. Bundled in the strong arms of smiling nurses, she was brought to me, while the other little ones were packed in a trolley. My daughter was showered with affection, and compliments, *"Che bella bambina."*

Thank God, my parents came to see us and my mum made me follow the rule and tradition of our culture.

In Somalia the extended family, mothers, sisters, aunties, grandmothers, cousins, even neighbours and friends take care of the new mother. They clean, cook, wash and go to the market for shopping. The new mother is pampered, special soups are cooked, she has to rest and have a lot of time to bond with her baby. For forty days she stays at home and goes out only for necessary reasons. Lots of guests come to the house, religious ceremonies take place and the kitchen is bubbling with pots and pans. Happy people come to greet the new member of the community.

My mum was very determined; she took care of the house and of my diet. You should see how desperate she was when she could not find *caano geel*, camel milk.

I lazed comfortably in that special atmosphere.

Ramadan

When one leaves one's own country and is trying to integrate in a new environment, so as not to be left out, it is very difficult to maintain one's own traditions. We were the only Muslim family in town. No mosques, no satellite television programmes. We would rely on the monthly prayer timetable sent to us by post by the Mosque in Rome and phone calls to and from friends and relatives to find out about big Islamic events.

Although my umbilical cord is firmly tied to my religion, in my daily routine, the month of Ramadan is the anchor. Fasting in Italy is like skiing on the desert dunes. Long working hours, solitude in returning home, unknown neighbours. Ramadan is a sacred month, where families reunite, pray together and break the fast with special foods. How funny we look, my husband and I, having the last meal of the day, sitting alone, in silence, before dawn, at the kitchen table.

Memories of my childhood flash in front of me like an old photo album: I am scrutinising the sky in search of the new moon, around me, my mum and dad, uncles and cousins, the whole neighbourhood. Magic is in the air, and excitement in guessing who will be the first one to spot the silver crescent. Then a chorus of blessing, "Welcome Ramadan!"

During the day, only the young ones have lunch. In the afternoon the cooking starts. The aroma of food floods the rooms: vegetables, chicken, and lentil soups, semolina. Beef and goat stew, spicy rice. *Buur*, sweet bread, *sambuus*, samosas, *bajiya*, fritter made from a paste of black-eyed peas, *sabaya*, Somali bread, *muufo*, millet and corn scones, *sukhar*, diced meat, *canjeero*, spongy and sour flatbread, *malawah*, sweet pancakes. Mothers telling their children, "Take this tray of *sambuus, muufo* and sweets to auntie; careful, don't drop it!"

Ramadan is the month of sharing, forgiving, emphasising, repenting, cheering, telling stories of the Prophets. Radios are stationed on Quran recitation. Girls are setting the tables, counting the last minutes before they can sit with the adults. Ice cubes are melting slowly in jugs full of lemonade and of fresh grapefruit juice. The sun sets, painting the sky with its last colours: orange, pink and violet. A cool breeze enters from open windows and patios. The call for prayer comes from a hoarse voice. It echoes and spreads from many minarets around the lively city.

This special month culminates with the celebration of *Eid-El-Fithr*. The night before came the preparations, the finishing touches to the new dress that all of we children must have, so that they compete on who have the best one. Little girls' hands are painted with henna, with drawings of flowers, stars and joyful motives.

The house smells of home-baked cakes; in the courtyard lambs bleat; they will be sacrificed the next day.

In the morning, the aroma of rice and spices mixes with songs and laughter. The mosques are filled with people, and after the prayer all of us children are free to run holding hands. We go from door to door, greeting everybody, "*Eid Mubark*, Happy Eid." Our neighbours offer us pastries filled with honey, sweets made of coconut and sesame, rose-scented red grenadine.

Love Dances

My mother's face, not young anymore, glows remembering her childhood. She would tell me stories, "When the rainy season starts, the savannah is lush and green, and every bush blossoms. My nomadic parents settle with their goats and camels. I play with Isha, my twin sister, and the other children. Many families from different clans get together and socialise. Wise men with grey beards chant past history and count dead animals from previous seasons. Handsome, strong men compose poetry for their sweethearts."

She told me these stories so many times that I felt I had been there. I could see the thorny bushes covered with yellow and purple flowers. The sweet smell of resin and acacia trees, the scent of the wet, red soil. Long legged, newborn camels suckle; black and white, shaven hair, with soft, pendant ears lambs bleat. Warm drops of rain fall at the equator, while young, statuesque figures dance, sing, clap hands and praise the beauty of maidens. Attractive, chaste girls cover their pointed bosoms, conceal their faces and hide their smiles, uncovering only their jaunty eyes.

It was amazing to see how these memories would change her. It was as if her mind woke up from a long hibernation. Softly, in a low voice she started to sing a song and her old body began to move slowly, with grace, at the rhythm of *Gabley-shimbir*, dance of the bird. Raising her limbs wrapped in pale colourful *garbasaar*, she would gently spread her arms like a flying bird. Her deep ebony eyes were dragging me into her magic world.

The Well

The sun rises early in the tropics; cool breezes and pink skies don't last long and soon the hot, salty air of the ocean makes me hide in the shade.

My mum always believed the opening of the day to be the best time to brush up a lesson, to memorize a poem, or to learn multiplication tables. So, as soon as I wake up, I must have a book in my hands for a few minutes. In the meantime, my *Nana* is preparing breakfast. Dad is listening to the news on the radio.

I love to sit on the cement steps that lead to our garden; that is my favourite spot. Old leafy *neem* trees, a blooming, white jasmine fence, a couple of tall papaya trees; one is male and sterile, and the other one is always bearing generously tasty gifts. From where I sit, the green oval-shaped fruits look like the big breasts of a pregnant woman.

In the corner, fragile branches embellished with green leaves look innocent, at least until you taste their fierce, tiny, red chillies: some wild cherry tomatoes, basil and bushes of purple periwinkle. A red oleander with burled branches stands like a passionate flamenco dancer. The wind carries lemon scent.

I am distracted by the hopping sparrows pecking crumbs, my charming turtle carrying her engraved shell in my direction when I call her. I can read only a few lines of the book I hold. Nature is magic and hard to resist, until the knocking on our gate reminds me that reading time is over.

Madina, our maid, has arrived. She is always the first person to enter our house. She carries fresh, hot rolls of bread straight from the *forno*, wrapped in newspaper. I like her. She has this special way of telling stories that make people laugh. My mum threatened many times to dismiss her, but she always kept her. The maid is untidy and forgets to do things around the house, but she is honest. Her life is complicated; she has a husband who falls in love with other women. Sometimes he spends his whole salary in gifts to court them, but he gets bored quickly.

Madina, in those days, loses weight, talks about him the whole time while she washes, cleans, sweeps and dusts the furniture frantically. She is a real 'drama queen'. Our friends like her too. She is ready with a spicy cup of tea or a cold drink as soon as they arrive. She knows the habits and moods of all of them.

One morning, Madina had a long face. She hurried into the kitchen and whispered something to my grandmother. I saw *Nana* shaking her head, saying, "May Allah have mercy on her!"

My mum was yelling at me, "Hurry up, you will be late for school."

My daily routine did not change, but the mood in our house was different for a few days. I was trying to grasp some information from the adults without being seen as I was not allowed to sit and listen when mum's friends were with her. So I went to Madina, "Who is the girl who died?"

"Gigia," she replied; there was astonishment in her voice, and her eyes looked far away.

"Gigia. That is why I did not hear her giggle coming from behind our fenced wall." I knew that people die and never come back. My mum went to funerals; after stripping off her golden earrings and rings, she always told me, "You have to show your sorrow even in the way you dress."

The name of the dead and their family are mentioned saying, "May Allah give them the patience and strength to endure their loss. To Allah we belong and to Him we shall return."

But with Gigia, it was as if people wanted to hide something. "Gigia, I saw her yesterday; she was not sick."

"Go away, you are just a little girl."

Madina was never so rude to me; she always had many things to tell me, but this time I was scared to ask any more questions.

Our house was on two floors and I liked to look from the window to see the girls passing by every day. They went to the well, carrying their *tungi*, clay jars, to fill them with drinkable water. Gigia was so lively, so talkative; wearing a *guuntino*, her bare shoulder looked so slim, yet so strong. She would pull the heavy bucket full of water fast, singing, and the other girls would follow her tune. She also filled the jars of the old women who came after her, making the ones in the queue angry. She was generous. She splashed water on her face to cool the heat. She showered her friends, making them run. The wet, cotton fabric stuck on her firm breasts: they were standing proudly, like young soldiers ready to conquer the world. She was not hiding her beauty. Life was bursting from every pore of her amber skin. Sometimes I used to run and open the gate to see her passing, and she would sprinkle water on me giggling. I would shout her name from the window, her reply a twinkle of pearls.

We did not know her family. They lived in the suburbs, where there was no running water from the tap: simple houses, half brick, half mud walls, covered with galvanized sheet metal. When big, warm raindrops hit strongly on those roofs, the wind would spread a drumming sound on the city. I would close my eyes and listen. The air was filled with an intense cocktail of scents of wet soil, tarmac, eucalyptus and acacia trees.

When I hear hasty steps, sounds of water and female voices, I open our gate to see if Gigia is back. No sign of her; the well is not the same. Although it is full of women, they are like shadows painted in grey, only buckets echoing in the deep hole, ropes rubbing on calloused hands.

My head is filled with words that have no meaning to me. Madina telling *Nana*, "She was found in a pool of blood, she has done it herself."

Our next door neighbour, rushing to us, "Have you heard? Nowadays, for those who have a daughter it is as if their shame were exposed. May Allah protect us."

Aunties, and visiting friends, repeating, "*Eeb*, shame, shame!"

"Why did she do that?"

"She looked like a nice girl."

"What shame on her family."

"You could tell she was naughty, by the way she giggled."

"Her eyes had that sparkle."

"She went too far."

"She provoked, and seduced."

"She was pregnant, could not hide it anymore."

"She used a knitting needle, alone."

I knew Gigia was not married, "Why are they talking about her having a baby?"

I did not have anybody to ask what really happened. In our city, people did not speak of blood and killings. The only blood I saw was the blood of a lamb or of a chicken when it was slaughtered. I could not imagine where the blood was coming from. I had nightmares of Gigia covered in blood, I would wake up sweating. When I asked my mum, "Why did Gigia have blood? How did she die?"

My mum hugged me and said, "*Hooyo adiga ilmo a tahai*, you are a little girl. Don't listen to adults talking; I don't want you to bring up this *sheeko*, matter, again."

Soon mum and *Nana* put an end to those talks. Gigia was forgotten. Nobody spoke about her. We never met any member of her family. It was not fun anymore for me to peep at the well; giggling voices did not reach our house.

I buried her memory, passing from childhood to adolescence, and finally reaching womanhood.

Novara is a cold and humid town, always blanketed by a dense fog. I am sitting on my cosy *divano*, wrapped in a red acrylic blanket, watching television.

On the screen, angry women protesting against the slaughter in back alleys, against clandestine abortion, against the suffering, the loneliness, the death, the persecution of the law.

Women want to get in charge of their bodies; they chanted the slogan, "*L'utero è mio e me lo gestisco io!*"

They want to have the legal right to decide what to do with what they carry in their wombs.

My mind shifts to a remote place, the sun is reflecting on a white city, sandy red dunes on the horizon, sound of water splashing, giggles, a forgotten face is smiling at me. Tears plough my memories; a bubbling girl, full of life, is holding my hand.

Far Away Lands

On cold, rainy, gloomy days when the icy wind blows on my contracted face, all of my body remembers the tropical land where I grew up.

A climate ruled by monsoon winds, from the northeast and southwest, with irregular rainfalls. I turn my thoughts to the hottest period between the changing of winds: *Tanga-m'-bili*.

I can see Mogadishu, romantic and drowsy. It is a city filled with the salty, marine air of the Indian Ocean, the scent of sweet, floral notes, musk, incense, houses with terraces and gardens brightened by the moon. It is a city where gossip is done without malice, where the long nights are full of imagination, and forbidden, passionate love. Curvaceous women, wrapped in colourful, transparent veils, possess enigmatic looks. Youths full of dreams and plans for the future; vitality that is weakened by the sweltering, oppressive, *Tanga-m'-bili* sticky heat. It is a city where time can flow without a clock. We live in the present and the future is in the hand of God.

At these familiar, vivid images, my muscles relax, my skin softens, and my whole body loosens; even the grey, heavy sky becomes clear.

I walk briskly, my shoulders are straight and I smile at a far land that I carry inside me.

Siesta

Coming to Italy I had to adapt to a different lifestyle. In Somalia, the weather regulates our daily routine. The day starts early in the morning, in schools, offices, shops and markets. At around two o'clock in the afternoon, businesses close. Soon after lunch the whole city slips into lethargy. The sun has no mercy. Everything stops! Even cats, dogs, birds, lizards, ants look for a place in the shade. Shutters are closed to keep the heat out. In the shadowy room our bodies search for each other; we love intensely, the way only the African land can allow. We sweat, our bodies and soul are at peace, and we sleep embracing.

Many years have passed. I am integrated to the Italian lifestyle. In summer, the suns rays inflame the air. The cement city and tarmac roads burst out hot wind, making it difficult to breathe. I am longing for my siesta, which gave life a wonderful taste.

PART THREE

Deep Nostalgia

When I was a young girl, I always travelled with my imagination, and my atlas. There was no Discovery Channel, low-cost flights or Google. I daydreamed of places I read about in a novel, a poem, an article. Movies took me to Rome, Paris, New York City. My dad used to bring home the *National Geographic* magazine full of images from faraway lands, like Australia, the North Pole, New Zealand, Japan, and their people.

When the big news, "Man sets foot on the moon", hit the world, my father followed the live radio broadcast, to make sure not to lose even one step of the memorable lunar landing, incredibly excited, like a child.

"It is not true, I do not believe it!" said my mum, the sceptic.

The following day the picture of the moon was on the newspaper, but I was not interested in it, as it reminded me of *gruyere* cheese, with all those big holes. I was happy to see my moon from afar, romantic and sometimes scary after watching a movie about werewolves.

I wanted to see the world, and so it happened. I visited medieval and gothic churches, walked ancient cities, India, Far and Middle Eastern lands; walked along the beaches of Caribbean islands, saw the sun go down and elephants march in the savannah. I have lived in Manhattan, considered the *ombelico del mondo*, but I could not smooth out the nostalgia for my Mogadishu.

The more I travelled, the more I came to realize that I carry inside me the precious cultural and historical heritage of my country. A piece of history that will never come back, and that I, like old African storytellers, will never stop telling.

Third World

Everything that is poor, ugly, dirty, backward, underdeveloped is classified as Third World. I have never liked this label; to put it on entire continents makes me feel bad.

In my travels, I discovered the Third World in Rome, Milan, Los Angeles, New York, London, Paris, where thousands of immigrants are confined in ghettos, leading a miserable life, a life often worse than the one they left behind when they moved to a new country, with the hope of improving their existences and those of the ones they love.

I am ashamed for the ones who think that the Third World is only in far lands, and continue to attach labels without realizing that intolerance and racism are creating a Third World in their own countries.

Southern Hemisphere

We lived in a flat, with a little balcony facing the street, like most Italians. There was no garden were children could play, only a small cemented area near the garages. In summer, boys would kick a ball, even if it was not allowed. I took my daughters daily for a stroll. We walked to the park and stopped in small *piazzas* to feed the pigeons. I felt there was not much space, just too many buildings; I could not see the sky. My mind would be elsewhere, surrounded by nature. I wanted to tell my little ones of big mango trees, camels, moving white clouds, foaming sea waves, but I did not say a word. They would not understand me. I felt they were missing something I could not give them. My husband and I were born in Africa. We had precious memories of our childhood, and we wanted our offspring to love that land. My spouse searched for a job abroad and, when he got the proposal to move to Zambia, we were thrilled.

Finally, the day of departure came; we boarded the plane with our luggage, a few dolls, an old ragged turtle and Samira's inseparable pillow. The flight would take long hours; Zambia is in the southern hemisphere of Africa.

"*Mamma* where are we going? Why are *nonno*, grandfather, and *nonna*, grandmother, not with us?"

Their tired legs were confined in rows of seats.

We adults had a lot of questions in our mind too. Zambia was very far from Somalia; it has no ocean, but it is on our continent. We were young, full of enthusiasm, and ready to go and start a new chapter in our lives.

After so many years, as a family, we still carry lovely memories. Africa imprinted my daughters' childhood; they remember our trips to vast safari parks, monkeys jumping on the jeep. The immense lake Kariba, they thought it was the sea. The sight of Victoria Falls took my breath away.

Playing in our extensive garden they picked up blackberries, bilberries and guavas, staining their dresses and faces, climbing up trees like squirrels, discovered grass snakes, scaring me. Green corn fields, where they would hunt for ladybirds. The clear, cold mornings, the breathtaking sunsets and the chilly evenings, when we would sit around the fireplace. Mango trees filled the air with their pungent scent, and we prepared mango juice in big pots. Ripe avocados would fall, and our cats would lick the fruit greedily. My daughters' English nursery school, with black tyres hanging in the playground used as swings, and their classmates, of different nationalities and skin colour. Going to the drive-in movies was a ritual: Salima and Samira would wear their pyjamas, carry their favourite toys, pillows, blankets. I would pack dinner. It was fun to sit and munch under the stars, watching the big screen, until they fell asleep.

Oh Lusaka! If I think of your nights, the sky full of stars, I live again the emotions I felt at that time: it was as if all the stars of the universe were there for me. It was like having a shower of stars, I forgot to be a grown up and became a child again. I wanted to touch the twinkling gems one by one. I felt as if each one were whispering magic words and rocking me in its spell.

Termini Station

Rome, *caput mundi*. I am at Termini train station, crowded with tourists, commuters, loud announcements. A cacophony of voices, people expecting friends and families. A group of nuns, students on school trips. A man playing the violin.

Everywhere I turn, I spot Somali faces: pretty, young and mature women dressed in jeans, skirts, trousers, T-shirts, long gowns, *dirac*, a traditional Somali women's dress, sandals and high heels, with the latest hair cuts; heads covered in colourful *garbasaar* or modest *hijabs*. Always in groups, to exorcise the solitude. Eyes perpetually searching for a familiar face, which has not be seen for a long time. Lips ready to smile at the first greeting, "*Sideed tahay? Wax cusub ma jiraan?*, How are you? Is there any news?"

Rivers of words flowing from the heart, the bad news is said quickly, as if to forget, and not feel the pain. They talk about the present and plan the future.

The Big Apple

When all my family went to live in the United States, in Manhattan, for me, it was a dream coming true. You could feel the envy in my husband's office colleagues, my daughters' friends, dripping from their lips.

I had the stereotyped images of Hollywood in mind, where everything is glamorous, and criminality is just a cinema exaggeration. The big American dream, according to which, in this mighty country, everything is possible and everybody can get rich and famous; you only need to work hard for it.

The big melting pot, millions of people from different parts of the world merging, getting the same opportunities, giving life to the nation.

I was part of the Big Apple, Manhattan, a jungle of cement. Skyscrapers that touched the clouds, long, parallel streets, traffic. Sidewalks crowded with people running, always busy. Sirens from police cars, fire engine and ambulances. Grey smoke coming out from road drains, as if it were a cry coming out from the deep belly of the earth, filled with people.

In summer, the subway is like a crematorium. People don't seem human anymore. On the corners of the avenues, men talking alone, some have only a dog as a friend; the elderly, wearing jogging suits, and young passers-by with headphones run, people who want to keep fit; a mad man carrying a big cross thinks he is Jesus, and wants to save the world.

Girls in mini skirts and dizzying heels. Boys carrying big radios on their shoulder, rap with hip-hop music in the air. Old folks rummage among garbage bins, tramps pushing supermarket trolleys full of empty cans, silent black limousines with dark windows slide on the roads.

Music and concerts, Shakespeare in Central Park. In summer, Cuban, Chinese, Andean and Moroccan rhythms burst at the Lincoln Centre.

You can taste food from all over the world in the restaurants of this city.

Autumn, the Indian summer, brings out the colours of the trees, makes you feel vibrant. The bay, the sea and the Statue of Liberty. Boats loaded with tourists, blowing wind that gets in the bones, the water is getting icy. Snow storms, tramps searching for heat crawl on the subway grating. Hurrying passers-by with cold looks, eyes avoiding any contact.

Living there, I realized that the American myth I had in mind was clashing with the reality. America and all its problems; a nation that had conflicts was unfolding in all its drama.

The big American dream, all that talking about democracy, seems to me a big hypocrisy. Injustice, poverty and racism were there in front of my eyes. The black ghettos are a crude fact in America. Poverty has lost its dignity; families break up. Black children nowadays have not seen cotton fields but live in cement towers where flowers don't grow. The white master did not snatch them from their mother to be sold. Many of them do not have a family; they never knew their father; many died of overdose or were killed by a bullet in a gang fight. Often their mother is thirteen-year-old; she is just a child, but she does not know how it is to be a child. All she knows is violence, abuse, shouting, beating. To these children, school is not prohibited like the times when it was only for whites. Now the doors of schools are open, and in those classrooms drug pushers do business.

Their eyes have not seen white men with a lash, but they know well the news cameras that show black men incarcerated. Fear of the violent, bad Negro man grows among the white population; it was useless to show young Rodney King, beaten and bleeding, in the hands of Los Angeles police.

The Hotel Porter

My husband travelled a lot on business. I convinced him to take me with him to Canada for a short trip. A taxi from the airport brought us to a hotel. A porter came to take our luggage. I noticed something familiar in his figure, the shape of his nose, eyes, the way he was walking. I tried to read his name written on the small brass plate of his jacket; I was right, he was Somali. "*Walaal sided tahay*, brother how are you?" I asked him.

His face opened with surprise and he smiled. Hassan told me his odyssey, how he bribed the policeman to get a passport, the journey on the plane, being a guest at a friend's place. Odd jobs, long awaited visas from different embassies. Time passing slowly and hopes vanishing.

Europe was not a good place for you; you could not find a job and you could not stay there. They did not want you. Finally, the refugee status was granted by Canada. Nomad's blood flows in your veins, but you travel without a camel.

You are now in Montreal, a large city. You have to adapt to walking on these streets, you have to learn how to fight that cold weather, but thank God, you do not have to be scared anymore.

I wanted to tell him: This is your home now. You look very handsome in your hotel uniform with all those big gold plated buttons. You do not have to think, only to smile, open and close doors, and so your mind is free to day dream.

Zanzibar

My dad used to tell me about Zanzibar, the island where he was born and brought up. In his older years, his memory became more vivid. He used to repeat often, "Your grandfather had clove plantations. In those days, it was a very precious spice. Men used to carry heavy bags full of *karafuu*, cloves, on their shoulders, singing while they loaded ships. Stone Town was like a jewel, made of white coral stones; the wooden doors were carved by hand. *Dhows* used to sail from the Arabic peninsula to trade, bringing lots of dates for the month of Ramadan.

At the palace of the Sultan *maa*, your grandmother, used to sing during festivities. On the day of his wedding, my brother looked like a *maharaja*: he was wearing a brocade jacket and an elegant turban while riding a red horse. The whole town was singing and dancing at the sound of an *oud*, a pear-shaped stringed instrument and the *tabla*, a percussion instrument.

… If I think about that funny incident, I feel like laughing again. I was a small boy when *maa* sent me to the cinema with a young house servant. As soon as he saw the image of a sea wave advancing towards him on the big screen, he ran away, screaming, "*Bahari na toka nje!* There is a tsunami!", and he left me alone in the dark.

Late in the afternoon we, like most families, would gather at the beach. Men strolled on the shore, ladies sat on the soft sand and the children were silent, waiting for this enormous ball of fire to be quickly swallowed by the sea."

In his childs eyes, this picture was stamped forever.

My father is buried in a small Italian cemetery, with no palm trees, only cold, marble gravestones. When I go to visit him, I try in vain to capture the sunset, but I can only hear the noise of the traffic from the nearby motorway.

I shut my eyes and think of him, his childhood, his island. The island of cloves, of coconut trees and white, sandy beaches. The island where people speak a melodious language, and music is a fusion of different cultures. Zanzibar, I have imagined you for years through my dad's stories. Zanzibar, when finally I met you, it was as if I had always known you.

I remember walking the narrow streets of the old town, sounds of children playing, laughing, running barefoot, soft footsteps like cats', men in long white *khamis*, robes, wearing beautiful *kofi*, skullcaps, talking while sipping *ka'hawa*, coffee, from small cups, sitting in their half empty shops. Radios playing *taarab* music. "*Allahu Akbar, Allahu Akbar*" the voice of the muezzin calling for the *ishaa*, evening prayer.

Zanzibar, I carry you inside me in these Western cities, grey, inhospitable, all looking the same, with the sound of traffic, and the smell of smog.

The Purse

I find this purse sleeping in a drawer under long, silky, colourful scarves, old coins, thin, stained paper money from a country that no longer exists, faded postcards, a broken silver chain, a huge, warm, amber bead necklace, ancient as its timeless past, a forgotten twig of an unknown tree, a hand-made skull cap that has lost its white brightness, tiny empty bottles that still preserve the oily scent of musk and jasmine, a worn wooden spoon, a light woollen red shawl, good for chilly summer nights.

My heart beats faster; the sadness I feel is covered, almost shrouded, by the breath of death. Tears to my eyes, I hold this little black purse.

The once young, shining leather is now opaque and smooth to the touch, covered in tiny grains, like wrinkles on an old face. These lines are the geographical map of a long story dear to me. I try to open it pulling its zip by the buckle. I don't have to struggle; it runs like a steam engine train on greased tracks. The inside is empty. The lining is made of a blue, cotton fabric. It is stained from the years of carrying pocket money to pay for short city trips in Fiat taxies, to buy fruits and vegetables piled in busy open markets, where the sun prematurely rots the delicate skin of round tomatoes and curved, tasty bananas, sending in the air a smell delicious to hungry silver winged flies. Small new notes to pay for fresh, fragrant bread. Copper coins that bring a smile to a crippled beggar and also to a dry mouthed child getting her favourite lemon ice lolly.

The contrast between the leather's black colour on the outside and the linen's deep blue of the inside drags me into this ocean of memories.

I am trapped, swimming in the depths of tropical water, crossed by sudden cold waves. I am scared to open my eyes. My life is entangled, embroiled like the enigmatic design sewn on this little purse.

I feel the love of my childhood, those eyes that could see me even from the back of her head. The tender sound of her voice, getting sharp to my childish whims. Her smile of approval at my small victories: when getting a good mark in Math, my hated subject in school, when being polite to scrutinising aunties at crowded weddings.

Her whole body singing of joy when she held for the first time my newborn. I can see her slim figure walking, cooking, laughing, crying, praying, washing, holding and helping friends and neighbours. I can see her handing a bunch of yellow roses brought for her by a nun in the hospital where she spent many days in the last year of her life.

This woman was not afraid of dying. She taught me how to respect life, but to be ready also to depart from it. How to have dignity and love humanity. She taught me how to carry on but not to forget my traditions, my language, my heritage. This little, black, handmade piece of art is my mother's purse.

Diani Beach - Mombasa

An evening, after having a creamy *risotto con funghi*, risotto with mushrooms, followed by a spicy chicken masala, we where ready to take out the photos we took on our last summer vacation. Looking at those images I found myself in Kenya.

Our *makuti*, roof made of palm tree leaves thatched together, bungalow on the beach, the *Masai* watchman wrapped in his red blanket, a bow and an arrow in his hands. The kind of folklore tourists love; I have fallen for it too. Our lullaby, the waves of the ocean, and the full moon our cover for the night.

Holding hands, walking on the white, clean sand, happy to be together.

At dawn, the sea is flat like an oil painting, the air fresh and salty. A man is bathing his camel.

The day starts to get brighter, the sun gets hot, the sea turns into indigo and emerald. We move fast on the burning sand, vendors all around us: women selling gaily coloured *kangas*, straw baskets, men holding polished, wooden statuettes of elephants, hippos, giraffe, masks, smiling faces. *Hakuna matata*, no problems at all, is the slogan in this area of the world. The tired camel is carrying an overweight blonde woman on its back, and a billboard advertising a restaurant is hanging on its side.

A lobster red couple, sitting on a boat; an old fisherman is rowing standing, his shoulder dripping with sweat.

It is sunset, our last footsteps on the wet sand, before the tide wipes everything away.

Madafu

Shopping in markets is always fun, especially when my dad and I were not actually going around with a shopping list. We were just walking around, filling our eyes with the atmosphere surrounding us. This is our vacation; we came to visit my grandmother in Mombasa.

I love coming to this town, my dad has time to spend with me. We do things differently than when we are in Mogadishu. Dad works the whole day there. When he is resting on the sofa, he always has a newspaper or a magazine to read; he is quiet. In the evening, we go to watch a movie. He seems a lonely person, he has few friends.

In Mombasa, my dad is another person, he seems happier to me. *Maa* spoils us, preparing all the Asian food he missed during the year. In the evening, after the prayer, we buy our dinner on auction at the mosque. Women at home prepare a dish and donate it as charity. The table is full of different dishes: chicken, lamb, prawns, vegetable *biryani, vindaloo* and *madras* currys, *parotha, nan, chapatti*, fried fish, *faluda* and homemade cakes. The auctioneer is a short, bald man who goes so fast that, if you are not quick enough to raise your hand, you risk that somebody else will buy the dish you wanted to purchase.

During the day we go to the seaside. Dad meets his old school mates they talk a lot. He laughs much more than he usually does. Sometimes I feel a bit left out, but I enjoy being with him.

At the market, the smell of dried fish is very strong; it makes me sick at first, but then I get used to it. We walk on the dusty road, stopping in the shade of the stalls.

The smells of guavas, oranges, pineapple and mangos are very penetrating now. A woman is selling roasted corn. Dad has two favourite stalls, the one which sells *chashew*, and the one on the corner of the street, where the market ends, and all the buses stop: there he is, the *madafu* seller.

A very dark man, deep-set eyes, skinny face; his long slim arms are so strong that you can see the muscle contracting, forming a lump under his skin. He is holding a sharp *panga*, machete, and chopping very fast the top edge of a large, green coconut. He makes a hole, and then he inserts a knife to scrape the tender, white fruit pulp. In that hot sun it is a relief when the tasty milk enters my mouth; I drink slowly and pull out long strings of meaty coconut to chew. Dad drinks more than one and says, "This is the best drink in the world when you are hot and sweaty, a cure-all."

The man replies, "*Kweli*, you are right", and continues chopping other coconuts. Behind him, a mountain of empty shells.

Then, I did not know it was an exotic fruit.

When I came to Europe in the hot summer days, I did not see *madafu* in the markets. I missed it. Then I went back to Mombasa and the taste had not changed. I found it in New York City, served as an Afro-American drink. In the joyful island of Cuba they spoil it with rum. At Cayman Brac, it's natural like its beaches. In Antigua it is served at the hotel by an elegant waiter wearing a tie. In Mumbai, on the promenade, you have to queue behind large families to buy one, paying a few *rupees*. On the beach in Goa, under the moon, the juice has the familiar taste I knew as a child. And, at last, in Zanzibar, the name has never changed; they all still call it *Madafu*.

PART FOUR

Somalia

Somalia. The Egyptians baptized you Land of the Gods, and the Queen of Sheba loved your incense and your myrrh. In 1333, Ibn Battuta in his travels described Mogadishu as a large city, rich with trade. There, fabrics were woven and then exported to Egypt and to other countries.

Somalia, land of trade with India and with China. You had your courts, your kings and your queens. The nomads wandered inland, free men with proud faces behind their caravans of camels.

Somalia, land of poets. Sufis and saints departed from your shores to spread the word of Allah until Vasco da Gama destroyed every last one of your sultanates, burning all that he could not take away with him.

Somalia, land of conquest. From that time on, no more trade. Your terrorised people fled inland. The European colonizers came and raped the land, sowing the seed of future horrors. After independence came dictatorships and puppet governments, convenient for the super-powers.

Somalia, my land. Now you have exploded; you could not carry on! Now you do not respect anything, not tradition, religion or tribe. Even nature is against you; it no longer rains, as if by punishment from the heavens. Men do not distinguish their brothers, their sisters, their children. With their *Kalashnikovs* in hand they feel like gods. They rob, pillage, rape and kill. They impair their senses with drugs. You have neither mother nor father anymore. You have no compassion for anything. You destroy your people, the future and the past.

Where are your thickets smelling of acacia, your blue-skied cities redolent with the scent of jasmine, your beautiful women, tall and sinuous, your smiling children gathered under the gaze of the *Moallim*, who teaches the Quran before any other language?

Somalia, do not forget that the true words of Allah are "Peace and brotherhood."

Somalia, my mother, land of love. So many emotions: compassion, hate, curiosity, as well as exploitation, political opportunism and self-interested ploys which stir the hearts of those who tread on your soil, but never true love!

But only those who have walked along your white beaches, swum in your warm ocean, fished in your immense sea, seen the sun come up over the forests, listened to the calls of your birds, admired the colours of your sky, heard the roar of your lions, the laughter of your hyenas, drunk the milk of your camels, smelled the perfume of your flowers and woods, danced to the sound of your drums, listened to the verses of your poets, those who have fallen in love under your star-filled sky and sweated under your burning sun can love you the way I love you!

The Camel Drivers

My maternal grandparents were nomads. My mother remembered her childhood with joy. She would talk of the camels they owned and of how proud her father was of them. Still today 70 percent of the Somali population live by herding, and for a nomadic family camels have been the symbol of wealth for millennia. These people have journeyed undisturbed alongside their camels and over a territory which is twice the size of Italy.

In the war for power between urbanized and politicised clans, the nomads are those who have suffered the most from the effects of this immense tragedy.

The old Warsame is one of these nomads. He has walked for days. His eyes have seen horrors for which he can find no reason or justification. His voice is our historical memory, "Since the beginning of time, we have been free to roam the bush in search of grazing fields for our herds; with our thick-lashed camels, our ebony-skinned men with long, strong legs and hair shaped like an umbrella; our black-eyed women, with smiles of pearl, amber skin, sensuous breasts, with the neck of giraffes and a regal bearing; our children, with smiles as radiant as our sun; and our old people, with wrinkled faces, each wrinkle a mark of experience that commands respect.

Now our herds have been destroyed, our men butchered, our old ones are at the end of their lives and our desperate children cry with empty, distended stomachs while our agonized women are sterile from hunger and wander, prey to madness."

Sacrilege

The mosque of Scek Sufi is one of the oldest in the city of Mogadishu. Its imposing walls rise up alongside the old port, and it has always been the destination of pilgrims. Tragically, a sacrilege has been committed within the walls of this holy place that will mark the history of our country with an indelible stain.

About thirty young women sought refuge in the large mosque of Scek Sufi. In vain. There was no respect for the sacred place. There was no respect for the young mothers, sisters, wives. All were repeatedly raped, tortured and violated by gangs of despicable men. The desecration took place in an atmosphere of inconceivable violence, never seen before. Not even the Quran could stop them. The cries, the begging, the screams of innocent young women were useless. These women were left with shame and fear, the feeling that their young bodies would never be pure again and that the horror they experienced could never be erased from their eyes.

War games

My favourite game as a child was hide-and-seek. I used to play with a group of same-aged children who lived in my neighbourhood; we would form a large circle and begin to play. Counting to the melody of a nursery rhyme that all the children knew, we were eliminated, one by one, until only the hunter remained. At this point the hunt began. How wonderful it was to look for the most unthinkable nooks in which to hide and to race breathlessly against the hunter who had found us in order to get back to the den first.

Today, however, Somali children do not play hide-and-seek; instead, they play war. On their small, wooden writing slates you can still read the faded verses of the Sura of the Quran, "...We implore You for help... Guide us along the right path."

These children recall the sharp voice of the old teacher scanning the short verses of the Quran while they, sitting cross-legged on the straw mats, would repeat the sacred words aloud. Every once in a while their inappropriate giggles would be interrupted by the teacher's stick. Today, however, their little hands are not blackened by the charcoal they use to write, but reddened with blood. Their little writing slates have become guns. The invocation of peace has become a message of death. So these children play war.

They are youths who have seen their parents killed in front of their very eyes and so have become warriors. They are the warrior children. They have called themselves *morian*: adolescents armed to the teeth and at the service of the various War Lords, who no longer control them. They pillage, kill, assault the convoys to survive and, with their cruel actions, disseminate terror and panic in a population already exhausted by civil war and by famine. They have no laws; they are the maddened cells of a defenceless system. They constantly chew *khat*, a stimulant, whose leaves take away hunger and keep them awake, in order to stay alert. They are desperate, alone in a world where not a crumb of compassion remains. And, in order to defend their male dignity, like in American movies, they pull the trigger and shoot.

And it is precisely to one of them that I want to address this letter:

Brother,
You, who destroy that which others have built with love; you, who have no respect for women, remember that you were born to a woman.

You, who kill for a bit of bread, remember that that bit of bread will not satisfy your hunger forever.

You, who believe you are strong because you have a gun on your shoulder, remember that the strength of a man lies in forgiving, rebuilding, sowing, irrigating, teaching, tending, working, sacrificing himself, praying, crying, procreating and loving.

Stop, brother, in the name of Merciful Allah, stop! Too much blood has been spilled in vain. Can't you see the innumerable dead around us, the misery and desperation in our homes? How much longer will you continue to be the angel of death?

The New Beirut

The stories and testimonies that I collect from the refugees I meet are haunting. Bandits, who enter homes to plunder and, not satisfied with taking everything away, rape the women before the eyes of helpless fathers, brothers, sons and husbands. Thieves specialized in taking apart the sheet-steel roofs from the most humble homes, the tiles from the richest homes, the electric cables in the streets, water pipes and telephone lines. Everything is looted in order to be sold across the border. Boats leave the country with the entire booty of a city in agony. The stories of Ahmed, Alia, Hawa, Dahir, Yusuf, Mumina, Abdi, Rukia and others have one common denominator: the feeling of being completely crushed.

Whoever had a car tried to leave the city, but they were stopped by armed men who confiscated the vehicles; common people were forced to acquire arms in order to defend themselves, priming that damned spiral of violence that has degenerated into anarchy. Basic resources became very scarce and the population was afraid to go out, even though there was no curfew. Everything was missing in the hospitals. The only way to obtain the medicine that had been hidden away was to pay. The enthusiasm and the joy over the expulsion of the dictator were a faded memory by now and, day after day, the nightmare of fratricidal war assumed more terrifying proportions.

I look at Mumina's marked face. Her eyes are two slits, and her thoughts absent. She is not young anymore; the Mogadishu of her youth is the same laughing Mogadishu that I carry in my heart, but her most recent memories are spoiled by the absurd and paradoxical situations created by the war. In the marketplaces vegetables have disappeared to give way to *khat* plants.

Dahir, on the other hand, smiles weakly, shaking his head. He observes the butt of the cigarette he holds between his fingers and recalls that it had reached the point where whoever wanted to smoke had to do so in secret. Bullets cost less than a pack of cigarettes, he says, and it was easier to find a machine gun than a steak. His words are as heavy as stones, "At night, the city was lit up by phosphorous bombs instead of electric current … The bodies in the streets weren't buried right away and became the meals of rats and stray dogs."

The ageless face of old Abdi, instead, is a silent mask. He thought that he had seen enough of life but now, among his memories, there is also room for an immense blue sky, the earth burned by the sun, the advancing desert, the carcasses of animals dead from hunger. Small human agglomerations, homes made of cardboard and rags, silent children with big eyes. This is the landscape that accompanies him on his journey towards the border in the hope of getting out of that hell. In the distance, one can make out the squalid refugee camps. Around them nothing has changed; the landscape is the same. There is hope that an aeroplane will bring something to eat.

One, ten, one thousand stories of human desperation. And yet there is always someone who benefits. The jackals. The human jackals who regardless of the colour of their skin, race, social class, religion, country of origin are all the same. They get rich off the misfortune of others. They take advantage of the stowaways at the border crossing; during a war they are always ready to make money on the black market with food and medicine. Arms trafficking, armed protection, fake papers, escapes to safety, everything to the tune of dollars and in the name of the money god. The dollar is now an international currency, and at whatever latitude you might find yourself, that is the only currency that will certainly be accepted.

The Innocent

It's dinnertime. For us, it is the most important time of the day. All the members of my family are gathered around the table. The television is on, as it is every evening and in every house. Its presence is now indisputable, but it does not take us away from our conversation about normal, everyday events when, suddenly, thousands of innocent-eyed, hollow-faced children with skeletal little bodies burst into our homes for a few seconds on the evening news.

Our table is laid out. Perhaps, in that moment, our children are being picky while those eyes that look at us from the screen seem to say, "I don't have any choice."

I feel a pang in my heart when I see my people so reduced. Sadness overcomes me and, in my mind, I again see the innumerable images of so many reports that every newspaper has published: snap-shots of children, women and old people, skeletal from hunger, with wrinkled faces and enormous eyes. Exactly like the one the television is showing right now. The camera freezes the images, and a momentary wave of indignation and compassion overcomes us when we watch them.

We are beautiful, white and our skin is smooth. Our bodies are muscular and our faces smiling, like the mineral water commercials show us. Those people, however, have no name, no story. They are only images, images of ghosts that do not belong to us.

I try to finish my dinner, but my stomach has tightened and my mind is far away. The news is over and the television, undaunted, airs some commercials. Summer is near, and images of golden beaches and tropical seas tempt our fantasy. So I think of all those glossy magazines that show naked bodies of women on their covers and, in the inserts, promise fast diets that will enable everyone to show off a slim and agile body on the beach.

So the body has become an object, something that is no longer a part of us. It is like an article of clothing that must always follow the latest style in order to fit into those high-cut swimsuits.

I realise bitterly that while millions of children are dying of hunger in the midst of general indifference in the Western world, millions of women on account of the myth of the female body are insecure and frustrated, and teenage girls are becoming anorexic. A market worth billions has come out of this collective insanity. One must get rid of excess fat at all costs and, for that reason, should not pay attention to prices.

"Why?", I then ask myself, "Why, in the same way that we are infected by that frenzy for corporal beauty, are we not overcome by an impulse that pushes us to save those who are dying of hunger?"

The only answer that I'm able to give myself is that, perhaps, the cause lies in our egocentrism. That must be it, because one of the greatest difficulties that I have encountered in adapting to the first world was the exasperated self-centeredness. In fact, what hit me about the industrial world, and what continues to disconcert me even today, is that we all, unknowingly, live in a box. It is a prefabricated box with too many labels and so unless we get out of this box and tear off those labels we will never be free from preconceptions. And this reminds me of the story of the poor little goldfish who continued to swim round in the glass bowl thinking he was swimming in the ocean.

The screaming detergent commercial, claiming that "It gets things so white that you can't get any whiter", brings me abruptly back to reality. Dinner is cold by now and my appetite is gone, but thank God the "toughest stain" stays with me.

Living in Waiting

I live in waiting.

From the day that war broke out in my country, all communications have been cut off.

I have no more news of my uncle and my cousin, and so, just as I do, my countrymen dispersed around the world to live, waiting.

It seems that all has stopped: no telephones, the postal services do not work, aeroplanes do not take off. It is as if we had fallen back into the Middle Ages.

The only fragmentary news that we receive comes, rebounding from mouth to mouth, from those fortunate ones who were able to abandon the country.

Drawing on these meagre fragments, conjectures and inferences are made trying to keep alive within us the hope for the survival of our loved ones.

And so I continue to live in waiting, contenting myself with the rare television images that tear my heart apart: hunger, death, ambushes, aid that arrives and aid that does not arrive.

After a few seconds, another story comes on, while I plunge into the darkness inhabited by my fears, my memories, and my hopes.

Pilgrims of the Past

It's night time. I am in Italy, in my house wrapped up in a deep silence. My daughters, in their bedroom, and my husband, next to me, are sleeping.

I am unable to sleep; the memories of the past crowd my mind, follow me like shadows almost as if to protect me from the daily reality that I experience through television.

I go over those places, now destroyed, homes damaged by war, abandoned.

Silent city, ghost city.

Only my thoughts bring back to life the sounds, the echo of whispered words, the colours, the faces of people in the neighbourhood, my parents, my friends, and my only, impassioned love; if it weren't for him, all that I have lived through would be like an ice castle, melting under the early sun.

The Exiles

While travelling around the world, I often meet countrymen, old classmates and friends with whom I grew up. They are now well integrated people in various countries, with wives or husbands of different nationalities.

I have met and had discussions with political exiles, spoken with students, made friends with families, also with mixed families, ex-embassy employees and businessmen. The reasons that drove each one of us to leave are varied; we all have a story behind us and plans for the future, but what is common to all of us is a deep nostalgia for our country and the desire to go back.

What characterises our diaspora is that it is not studied in history books or documented by famous movie directors but has been experienced for more than twenty years in silence, almost covertly, but with dignified pride.

An invisible people's pride and dignity, pride that I have seen in many men and women whom I met in Jeddah, Saudi Arabia. In the early eighties, for my husband's work, we lived for many years in that country. It was in Jeddah, where the largest Somali community of the Arab Gulf states lives, that I met people reduced to do the humblest jobs, driven to emigrate by a serious employment crisis caused by the mad politics of the regime. The poor wretches were forced to make enormous sacrifices in order to be able to send money back to that land to which they hoped one day to return.

Just as these people did, other exiles made sacrifices. Saving to the last cent, many were able to build a small house in the middle of bushes of jasmine flowers. A house that, however, the war has now destroyed. Along with the homes, hopes were destroyed, families have been scattered, the panic of facing not ever being together again has spread, and the dream of repatriation has become unattainable.

Among those who were able to escape, the most fortunate are those who, after long and expensive bureaucratic procedures paid in hard currency received from abroad, have reached relatives in exile.

The less fortunate are those human beings who are forgotten in enormous parking lots placed at the borders of the Somali territory. All public opinion is focused on Mogadishu, but in these squalid, miserable refugee camps, like in concentration camps, people continue to die. Behind the barbed wire lie thousands of hovels made of rags and plastic to protect those neglected bodies from the infernal heat, and the only well, now inadequate, vomits a reddish-brown liquid. In this silent city, children do not play or smile anymore and at sunset people kill each other for a fistful of rice.

Fortune has been kind to Eugenio Yusuf, however. In fact, we received news that our old family friend had been able to get to Italy. After calling around we were able to get a hold of him, and when we spoke on the phone for the first time it was very emotional for both of us. He came to pay a visit and we talked for hours. His voice betrayed no emotion. Eugenio has always been a self-confident man, and he seemed not to have lost that quality. He told us that his flight was made possible thanks to his life savings and the invaluable help of some Franciscan monks who had lived in Somalia in previous years. He now lives in Milan as a guest in a monastery and is trying to repay the monks for their help in getting an entry visa by doing odd jobs for the order. Eugenio has always worked in a hospital as an analyst and chose not to marry. In his view, a good book, classical music, and a cheery gathering of old friends made up for this solitude, while in my mind I always suspected him of being something of a misogynist.

In all these years, he had never wanted to leave the country. He told us that it was the war and the madness of men that had driven him to come to that decision. He had now seen too many horrible things. The conversation continued with an exchange of information and updates on mutual acquaintances and friends that we had not seen for years. We call this way of ours of exchanging news Bush Radio.

During our gatherings, a desire to speak for hours in our language is triggered, a need to remind everyone of different things, even the flavour of foods. So we end up cooking our traditional dishes. We focus on the situation of friends we have not seen for years. We update each other. We dream of our return… And we ask ourselves painfully how we got here… For us, these gatherings are a full immersion into memory; they give us a charge that reawakens our African consciousness.

It was thus that in the course of our conversation I asked him if he had brought any pictures with him. He looked at me as if I were from a different planet and responded, trying to control his tone of voice, "I destroyed them all. What are photographs good for? For suffering every time I look at them?" and he added, "The memories that I carry inside me are already enough. I want to cut off the past."

Those words struck me. His reasoning was flawless, but it was done from a perspective that I personally had never considered. I looked at him and it was as if I were seeing him for the first time. I asked myself how a sixty-year-old man would want to forget his whole life.

I understood the desperation that was in that man. I was unable to hold back, and in order not to embarrass him I got up and left to cry.

Eugenio has closed himself up; he does not meet many people and disclaims the external world. He says that in Milan everyone is crazy, always running, traffic scares him, the sky can't be seen, the stars don't shine and the sun doesn't have the time to smile.

Hussein

Hussein's parents have now been living in Italy for about a year. They are desperately seeking to mend their dreams by clinging to their two small children, who fortunately survived.

Coming to Italy was not easy. Their relatives toiled greatly in our country for many years in order to get them an entry visa.

Hussein was only ten years old. He was a healthy, strong, intelligent child, with a future ahead of him. How many times had he played the game of "When I grow up I want to be … a doctor, a pilot, a mechanic, a journalist."

Then a grenade blew up on his house. He died before his parents' and his relatives' eyes. And along with him died their hopes, their dreams, in a war without any real winner.

PART FIVE

African Heart

When I first came to Italy in the early seventies, people would ask me, "Where are you from?" I used to say, "Mogadishu, Somalia." They did not know much about my country.

Today in 1993 the name Mogadishu will bring to mind another African nation where an everlasting war goes on, dead bodies litter the streets, anarchy and boys under fifteen carrying *kalashnikovs*, a country where people die of hunger.

The usual Africa, the one the Western world identifies with famine, images of undernourished children with no name, clans killing each other, drought and desperation.

My African heart bleeds and screams in pain, but it is a silent scream. Now I would like to say out loud that Africa is a continent full of resources, generous, rich in humanity. You have to live there with its people to be touched by its generosity and sharing.

You have to see the colours of its lands, its scent, its sounds, the sense of absolute freedom that its immense spaces inspire. Its songs, beaches, savannahs, bushes, sunsets, the sound of the African nights, skies full of stars, dawns, the cheerfulness of the people, the wonderful eyes of children hanging from their mothers' shoulders.

I would like to shout at this big continent, "Wake up ill giant! Although they have caused you pain by wrenching away your offspring, selling them as slaves, exploiting your riches with the excuse they came to civilize you, imposing on you an economic system that ties you without chains and then... war, hunger and famine. I know that, in the end, you can make it. Wake up ill giant!"

My heart bleeds, but I am optimistic. These wars will end. After colonialism and dictatorships that are now collapsing, a new Africa will rise.

I am proud to have been born in Mogadishu, to have an African background and to be a Muslim. I have been living abroad for many years, but the years spent in my country gave me great sensitivity and a heart that no other culture can destroy.

My optimism does not blind me. The racism, the selfishness and the lack of understanding towards an emigrant who wants to better his or her life frighten me more than the images of war and famine.

Cultural Leftovers

In my country there was a fertilizer factory that had never produced anything; electricity, petrol and the personnel were missing. So, with the sun and the salt deposit it rusted, and at last, one day, it was dismantled and sold as scrap-iron.

There was a project for the master plan of Mogadishu, which cost billions but was never accomplished and, as it passed from the hands of one famous Italian architect to another, the potholes in the streets of the capital became chasms. The sewage system remained non-existent and slums sprang up like mushrooms, side by side with the luxury villas complete with guards.

There was a tannery entrusted to a well-known Italian fashion designer that produced nothing. There were a sugar factory and a food factory left unfinished. There was a road in the desert that has never been used for civil purposes... and I could go on.

I, as an Italian citizen of Somali origin, feel doubly cheated by the long years of 'Cooperation and help to Somalia'. I can understand the taxpayers' anger when they find out that their money, administered under the umbrella of cooperation, ended up in useless projects, wastage, bribes and corruption.

I am a taxpayer and I feel I deserve clarity and I want justice. As a Somali, I feel I have been used, as have my fellow countrymen, without our country benefiting.

After this outburst let me consider the reality. Billions have been spent, but what remains of Italy are *caffè espresso* and the love for *spaghetti* and *pizza napoletana*.

The Pharisees and Mother Teresa

Every time I see thousands of children exhausted from hunger, I weep with rage. I feel anger towards those infamous politicians who did not intervene earlier in this drama but waited until it became a tragedy. I hate these games of interest that are made at the expense of innocent children, of a defenceless people.

But how do you fight the system when the power is with the executioner who masquerades as a benefactor and who, in the end, ironically, we must also thank?

And that is when my thoughts turn to Mother Teresa of Calcutta. She is one of the female figures I most admire. That little old woman, wrapped in her simple white *saree*, her eyes smiling and shining with love. It is with her name that I want to ideally identify all the unnamed Somali mothers we see in the magazines and on the TV screens in our houses.

Therefore 'my' Mother Teresa has black skin and a sunken face, but she has not lost the regal and proud features of her people. Her eyes are large, black and hold all the horror of holocaust. To her breast, once lush and sensual, is now attached a large-mouthed child with a huge head and a swollen belly. From her breast, not a drop of milk comes out, arid like that land where it does not rain for months and, as if it were not enough, men unleash their madness: men, who think they can make it fertile with the blood of their enemy. They do not understand that bloodshed is not life, that love is needed, like the love I see in Mother Teresa's eyes for her children.

Neologisms and Hypocrisies

The first time I heard *vu cumprá* (you want to buy?) I was shocked. I remember when, some years ago, school kids on buses turned to young Africans calling them Kunta Kinte, taking this expression from the TV series *Roots*. Many of those immigrants did not have the faintest idea what Kunta Kinte might have meant but now, thanks to the media, the term *vu cumprá* has become of current use. Everybody uses it, without thinking about how the person to whom it is directed must feel.

Faruk, an acquaintance of ours, who has been in Italy for several years and has fully mastered the Italian language, still cannot adapt to this habit of labelling everything and everyone. Once he asked me why the Americans and the Japanese are not called *extra-comunitari*. After all, they too are not part of the European community, but nobody would dream of calling them that. For some unknown reason, he added, in Italy every North-African has to be a *marocchino* or every African an *extra-comunitario*, Negro, Black, or *vu cumprá*.

Honestly, I have not been able to provide him with an answer, because I had already asked the same questions earlier, receiving only the justification of linguistic simplification. But these terms are dehumanising because, in this way, all the Africans remain a black, distant and uniform mass of non-persons.

I always thought that the measure of a country's civilization is not in its economic wealth, or in its own people elegantly dressed in designer clothes, but in the way this country treats its guests, since it is only the memory of the people met that remains in the hearts of those who return to their homeland.

The Suitcase

I am with a friend in a department store; we are in the luggage department. Sonia is looking for a suitcase. She is going to Tunis, a holiday that she booked last winter. All those bright coloured suitcases, bags and travelling bags take our minds to golden beaches, a blue sea and coconut palm trees. Sonia picks up a flashy red Samsonite, asking me, "Do you like it? Does it seem too big to you?"

"I like the colour."

We open it and Sonia starts to make a list of all the things she will need: hairdryer, sun cream, flip-flops… and all the objects she is going to take with her. Naturally, she has to leave space for souvenirs.

I look at her and realize that she is a lucky woman. Yes, because she never had to leave her country for economic, political, religious or ethnic reasons. She cannot understand the one who leaves behind loved ones, family, home, customs, land, ceremonies, feast days, songs, music, seasons, the dead, funeral rites, and religious ceremonies.

An immigrant has to fit all this into a very small suitcase.

Africa

Black soul, black day, black book, black hole, black cat, black heart, black beast, black sheep, black future, black comedy, black widow.

Why is black only seen as negative?

And yet, dark is the night that leads me to dream, black is the sky full of stars, the calm ocean in the night. Your beauty carved in ebony, your eyes full of love, dark the womb that gave me life.

Africa, immense are your rivers; your deserts advance inexorably. Your great outdoors, your fish-rich coasts, your villages lost in time, your unique forests, rich in life and of extraordinary beauty, your land and its fields of precious metals, diamonds and black gold. And man finds himself only when he loses himself in your womb.

PART SIX

A Special Day

Together with a few labour unions and some associations of foreigners we have been able to organize an event in my city for Labour Day. It was our first cultural event and our budget was very tight. The *piazza* was lively, stalls selling African crafts, books, musical instruments, food, bags, sandals; men and women dressed in traditional colourful clothes.

Piazza dei Signori, for one day, was animated by the rhythm of African drums, voices, colours; sensual bodies of magical ladies danced and brought warmth to the stern and cold heart of Vicenza, taking me back to the far lands where I kept the joy of living.

And, as night fell, the moon looked out, smiling, transforming the porticos into caves, and I could hear the echo of the sea waves lapping on my memories.

Fantastic Destinations

My little girl was five years old when, for the first time, she asked with her bright and curious eyes, "Mum, what was your school like?"

Many years have passed since that day. My hometown has been destroyed by bombs. Bombs that erased the places of my childhood, places that I always hoped, one day, to show to my two daughters. Now I can only write to them about these places, sharing with them an imaginary journey to fantastic destinations…

I wanted to take you to Gezira where the sand is so white and the sea so green, blue and clear that no poet can describe it.

I wanted you to lie down on the terrace of my house on a full moonlit night to count the stars and, during the day, to play with the clouds that turn and take you off to a fantasy.

I wanted to show you my old school, Regina Elena, where the scent of frangipani that grows in the garden is so strong that it floats into the classrooms.

I wanted to go with you to via Roma, the first road I knew and which was my whole world as a child: my tailor, my sweet shop, the mirror shop and the bar Leon d'Oro. The fabric shop, where silks from India were sold, Patria's Superstore, the pharmacy of Ali Bin Quer and the voices of all those people who greeted us warmly.

I wanted to take you to the Supercinema where, with great emotion, I saw the movie *Gone With The Wind* under the big starry sky.

I wanted to take you to the pastry shop of my childhood, where I ate the most delicious cakes ever.

I wanted you to enjoy the fresh shade under the big tamarind tree, to have a taste from the mountains of dates and to smell the thousand scents of exotic spices.

I wanted to show you the fruit and vegetable market held under the tall trees of the *piazza*, where goats and chickens ran freely.

I wanted to take you to the gold district, through the narrow alleys and small winding streets. To walk past the Great Mosque and climb the steps to the beautiful Cathedral, stopping at the gardens around the Triumphal Arch where we used to be taken as children to play.

I wanted to follow the curve that leads to the old post office building, where you can see the sea waves breaking on the rocks or admire the lacy brickwork of the Sultan's white castle, turned into a museum.

I wanted to take you to the old lighthouse and to show you the characteristic Shingani district, with its houses that resemble Portuguese fortresses.

I wanted to take you to the road that leads to the airport and roll down the sand dunes.

I wanted… but I cannot, because everything has been destroyed by bombs!

Children

Like in a fairytale, in the numerous Somali villages children would recite the Quran, play hide and seek, run after goats. They would smile, hanging from their mother's back, and sleep, cradled by the movement of her body while she pounded wheat. They would drink from a wooden bowl a white dense liquid, just milked, and when the sky became dark, letting the first stars twinkle, with wide-open eyes they would listen to tales of the bush, populated by lions, jackals, ostrich, gazelles, while they could hear the hyenas laughing and dancing in circles.

Like in all fairytales, an evil witch came and, with a spell, brought death, famine, destruction. These children are waiting for the spell to break and for everything to smile as before.

Silent Warrior Women

My work in the Somali community brings me into contact with many of my fellow countrywomen; I try to make them aware of their rights as women working in a society that only tries to exploit them.

They are for the most part women who left their countries in the hope of finding, through emigration, the opportunity to financially help their own families. They are young women who worked in government offices as clerks or telephone operators, or as teachers or nurses, and whose salaries were not enough because inflation had reached frightening levels. After emigrating, however, the only opportunity offered to them was to work as cleaning women. Their situation worsened with the war. All this because their relatives were forced to flee and abandon everything and are now refugees living in Djibouti, Ethiopia or Kenya. There, parents and children, uncles, aunts and cousins live with the uncertainty of their repatriation, counting however on the remittances that these brave women send them every month.

Amina arrived in Italy with a degree in nursing, but it was not recognized by the authorities, so she would have to re-enrol on an Italian program that lasts three years. She would like to do it, she has assured me several times, but it is impossible. Who would send money to her old father and to her little brothers? She is the only person in a position to help them and, consequently, she cannot escape her duty. So her aspiration to work in a hospital becomes a dream locked in a drawer.

I consider Amina and all the young women in the same situation to be fighters. I have named them the Silent Warrior Women. When I meet them, I cannot but admire their courage, their perseverance, the way in which they conceal their loneliness. The way they sacrifice themselves, but not for a career.

Their work is modest. They assist and take care of old women or look after spoilt brats. They wash, clean, tidy up and cook within the solitude of domestic walls, in a house that is not theirs. Their faces are smiling masks, but their deep black eyes are filled with melancholy.

The New Poor

In Italy we are going through difficult times. The needy are on the increase. Economic crises and people losing jobs are topics discussed among families. These are not only news items from the media, but also people with names and faces; some are acquaintances, others our friends. And so wars and desperation of other nations become distant. Somewhere between a joke and a serious comment people say, "I am tired of your wars, of your poverty, of your chronic hunger; the fact that you kill each other among tribes, like savages! I have my own problems: Mafia, corruption, Amato's government with all its economic reforms and cuts. I do not know if I will be laid off or dismissed, but I do know my thirteenth month's salary will be reduced. I feel poorer myself and I do not want to hear about how poor other people are!"

Do You Like Italy?

A question that has recurred since my first days in Italy and that many ask me, even today, is, "Do you like Italy?"

The inevitable next question follows my affirmative answer, "Do you prefer to live here or in your country?"

The first few times, I remained speechless. I felt almost hurt. With time, I made a habit of creating a barrier that protected me. Then I would respond with a smile, with an ironic comment and, depending on whom I was with, I would turn the question around.

Why do people not think before asking such idiotic questions? These people do not understand and cannot remotely imagine the pain that one feels upon leaving one's country.

When you emigrate, you do it because it is a forced choice.

I am an Italian citizen; I participate in and experience the problems, the suffering that all Italians face every day. I contribute to the life and the evolution of this country. Now that both my parents are buried here, I feel even more tied to this land. Italy is my home; my relationships are here, my friends. Even so, there is always someone who reminds me that I am an intruder, an anomaly.

When I return from one of my trips abroad, all the enthusiasm of finally coming home vanishes when I hand my passport to the customs officer who, almost surprised to find himself facing an Italian with dark skin, checks the document over and down to the smallest detail with a serious look, verifying its authenticity on the computer and checking that my name does not appear on the wanted list. Then he calmly hands it back to me with that haughty air painted on his face that, by now, I have learnt to know very well.

Or when I walk through my city and I read graffiti such as "Negroes out", "Go home"; or when we receive insults that if all goes well just end there, but may, in the worst cases, end in episodes of true racial violence. I rebel against this barbarism. The world is moving towards a multiracial society, and people need to realize that this process is unstoppable.

The Love Piano

It is a beautiful sunny day; my friend Muna takes her son Michele out. Pushing the pram towards the central piazza of Vicenza, she checks the little face that peeps from under the blanket to see if he is still sleeping. She is in the heart of the historical city; around her, priceless artistic palaces. It is a meeting point where people stroll; mothers let their children run and feed pigeons. A man sells birdseed. Muna stops to enjoy the warm spring day, two silver-haired ladies approach her and peep into the pram.

"*Che bel puteo!*" says the one with the blue jacket. "He is my first born." Muna is very proud.

The women look at each other astonished, then one says to her friend, "Is it true?" and they carry on, ignoring her.

Only then Muna realizes that they have taken her for the baby-sitter; Michele is very fair.

Obviously, for those two, it was not possible for an African woman to give birth to a white child. Muna was so angry at first but then, after some time, she told this episode doing an impression of them, making us laugh.

There are many children like Michele in the world and if we would let them talk, they would say, "Blue are the eyes that smiled at me, black the breast that fed me, white the hand that held me, black the womb that gave me life. Black or white, I do not distinguish between colours. I have been brought up with love and without prejudice. I speak both languages; I am the bridge that unites the two worlds. Many fear me, I know their soul. I am a chameleon; white-black, black-white; I am the one others cannot be. I fuse both cultures. I am free, the world is my home and my horizons are endless."

PART SEVEN

Airports

I have always had a weakness for airports. I experience a sense of euphoria before departure. Knowing that in a few hours, I can move from one continent to another is extraordinary.

I was five years old when, I fastened my seat belt on a plane for the first time. I remember that sense of power and emptiness in the stomach, knowing I could touch the clouds. The air hostess with big blue eyes is smiling at me; she is very beautiful, offering a tray where I dip my hand and pick up sweets wrapped in colourful paper.

I was very privileged, a little girl born in Africa travelling by air in the sixties. It was very expensive and most of my friends envied me.

Times has changed, low-cost flights are common and people are treated as goods. Pressed like sardines, we have to keep quiet, not even deserving a smile from the flight attendants. This attitude did not change my love for travelling by plane. I do not like trains, I get bored. The view I get from the windows depresses me. Suburbs of big cities: tall cement towers, houses like boxes, grey skies. Around me, sad commuters, sleepy students with dandruff in their hair: it is not a scene that gives joy.

Yet my best and unforgettable journey was when my dad and I left Nairobi on a train, whistling at the departure, to go to Mombasa. We spent the whole night travelling. We had our private cabin with white bed sheets, coarse woollen blankets, soft pillows and a small sink.

The night was cold and the moon was hiding, I was watching the train turning in the valleys and saw only the lights of the other windows. Small dots in the darkness, I imagined it to be a dragon's tail. The cabins were moving noisily and shaking, like big cradles rocked by a giant's hand.

In the morning a smart waiter in a burgundy uniform with golden buttons walked past our cabin ringing a silver bell and served us breakfast: eggs, toast, jam, butter and a hot cup of the best Kenyan tea.

Dawn came in silently from the window. The colours of Africa were painting the scene. I could witness the savannah waking up. The train was not going fast. The chilly air of the morning got warmer as soon as we found ourselves closer to the coast.

Passing through villages, huge mud huts with grass roofs that blended in with the lush green plantations of banana and maize. High palm trees kissed by the golden sun. Elephants and zebras grazing undisturbed.

Tall slim elegant giraffes walking under thorny acacia trees looking like models on a catwalk.

Tiny happy arms waving at us. Dignified women carrying bundles of wood on their heads, wearing colourful *kangas* around their waist.

Intangible dust full of life, bringing in the scent of an archaic, pure and beautiful world into our moving sitting room.

Travelling on modern air-conditioned *Freccia Argento* and *Freccia Rossa* could never give me any excitement.

Definitely, for me, it is better to travel by plane, even though the euphoria I once used to feel has been replaced by a sense of anxiety. Not really anxiety, I would probably say discomfort. I know my travelling documents will be examined carefully. It is not enough that my fingerprints are stored in a microchip in my passport, that I am a European citizen. The police woman will search my headscarf and her nails will touch my scalp. She makes me feel guilty for something I have not done by the way she body searches me.

I am in favour of security checks in airports but they should not stigmatise a religious group. Muslims have become scapegoats without committing any crime.

Airports are plasticised places, anonymous, looking the same all around the world. I would say they are huge shopping centres, where the passengers' only duty is to spend money. Everything is for sale, from cars to lingerie.

When I noticed the sign saying Prayer Room, I could not believe my eyes. I was not in the Middle East, but in the country of Tony Blair.

I walked in the direction of the prayer room. I looked around me skeptical to see if there were any CCTV-cameras or police chasing me.

Is it a trap? Are they going to search me more carefully if they find out that I have used this room?

I do not care, the desire to discover this oasis of spirituality is very strong.

I open the door, switch on the lights and take off my shoes. This large rectangular room feels cold with the neon lights, and its bareness is not inviting at first. I look around me; there are three sections.

In one area there are two rows of benches, a cross hanging on the wall and a simple altar with a Bible. The middle part is occupied by a table covered by a white tablecloth and on it there is a Menorah, the typical Jewish candleholder. The right wing is separated from the rest of the room by a light curtain and there I find some prayer mats and copies of the Quran.

I enter the *wudu*-room and turn on the tap for the ablution. I start washing my hands, rinse my mouth, nose, face, arms; a sense of peace invades my body, making me forget where I am. I do not know how many people have prayed in this space, but I can feel the holiness and sincerity of the travellers who came before me.

Alone in this spacious room with white walls, I take a folded mat and spread it on the floor, facing the *Qibla*; my heart, full of gratitude, begins to recite:

> *In the name of Allah, the All-Merciful, the Most Kind*
> *Praise is for Allah, Master of the Universe*
> *The All-Merciful, the Most Kind*
> *King of the Day of Judgement.*
> *You are the One we worship O Allah; You are the One we ask for help.*
> *Show us the Straight Path;*
> *The Path of those whom You are pleased with-not the path of those who deserve Your anger, nor of those gone astray.*

Leila

I remembered the words of the poet Gezim Hajdari, "It always rains in this country, maybe because I am foreigner".

It is July and the rain follows me everywhere. Not summer storms, but drizzly rain that slips down my body and gets in the bones. It seems like autumn; the sky is dark and grey in contrast with the light cotton dresses, mini skirts and T-shirts the girls are wearing. Elegant shop windows are displaying lovely stylish summery clothing.

I ask myself, "Are they going to sell these garments with this weather? Who is going to wear them?"

A flash of sun is covered by clouds carrying rain. Selfishly, I think it is better for me to have this chilly weather rather than the oppressive Italian heat.

I am in this city not as a tourist, but to live here. Something I had not planned. In my experience of moving around the world, I came to the conclusion that, at least for me, it is the cities that choose me. I have lived in places that I did not know existed.

Now I do not have time for these philosophical thoughts, I have to quickly resolve practical problems. I am looking for a house. There are many estate agents. There is no lack of houses on the market, but I have to find the best accommodation for my family.

I have lots of appointments, many properties to visit. Luckily the agents drive me, if I had to search for the addresses in the miserable weather, I would go mad. I had to learn and codify terms like: semi-detached, flat, detached house, terraced house, house, maisonette, bungalow, town house, penthouse, cul-de-sac.

The classical red-brick houses fascinate me, but there is a big difference between seeing them from the outside and visiting them from the inside; tacky wallpaper, horrible carpets, claustrophobic toilets and fake fireplaces are my nightmare.

I feel frustrated, but my optimistic side prevails. I do not give up and look for the home whose price coincides with my budget, and that gives me a sense of security and serenity.

Some neighbourhoods are so squalid, just a row of ugly houses with piles of old rubbish; worn out sofas, yellowish patched mattresses with popping out springs, broken bookshelves and ripped black bags dumped outside, dirty roads, not a single tree or flower pot.

Entering a new place I embrace the empty walls and try to feel their breath, looking for the feeling of homecoming from a new building. Like when you take a liking to a person you have just met.

Once I read that transfers and moves to a new environment are among the most stressful experiences you can have.

Maybe I have developed an antivirus due to the nomadic life style of my ancestors from the Horn of Africa.

Changes always challenge me. I love discovering new neighbourhoods, learning different languages and making new friends. It is the first few moments that give me strong emotions, the memories that will stay with me forever.

It is Sunday; letting agencies are closed, so I decide to behave like a tourist.

It is raining, but the people do not seem to be bothered, some do not carry umbrellas. I am trying to do the same, but it is difficult. I want to mingle with the crowd and ignore the constant voices of my internal radio, always ready to make comparisons with other cities. I want to flow with the people around me, like a river that flows lazily through the forest.

A huge bronze bull and a stunning cathedral surprise me. The architectural contrast of this metropolis with its navigable canals, the tranquil walking pace of its inhabitants, its pedestrian areas embellished with cascades of red, violet and yellow petunias. The gigantic modern statues and its attractive fountains relax me.

I reach the Sunday Market, everything is for sale: new and old mobile phones, silk Indian saris, antique and modern furniture, shoes, bags, household appliances, even stuffed toys that once belonged to naughty children.

Men with thick beards and moustaches, their long hair concealed in tight turbans, young and old white bodies painted with fancy tattoos, black men with grey dreadlocks hanging to their shoulders, babies strapped in their strollers, slim, elegant females draped in black material, only a pair of brown-green eyes allowed to be shown to the world. A cluster of people from every corner of the planet.

I clearly understand the language someone is speaking behind me. I slow down, they overtake me; it is a family. I just could not resist shouting, "Are you Italians?"

The lady stops, turns around; she looks surprised, her black olive eyes wide open, a smile hanging on her face, "Yes, we're Italians. Where do you come from?"

"Vicenza," I reply getting close to her.

"We used to live in Alte Ceccate, near Vicenza."

The coincidence surprises us more.

She points at her two adolescent boys, "They were born in Italy. Five years ago my husband lost his job and we moved to the UK. This one was born here," she says, touching the little girl's head.

Instinctively, we hug each other under our umbrellas.

"So nice to hear you speaking Italian. If you want we could meet, I'm new in town."

"Yes, I'd be very happy to, I have no one here who speaks Italian. Let me give you my phone number."

We take out our mobile phones to exchange numbers.

"What is your name?" I ask her.

"Leila, I am from Morocco. We often go to Italy for our holidays, my family live there. And you?"

"Habiba, I was born in Mogadishu".

I look at her, her eyes are sparkling; she has a radiant smile.

The rain is falling; we cannot stand chatting for long. We say farewell hugging and kissing three times on the cheeks, promising to meet soon.

The Wedding

I am in London for a short holiday. I love this multicultural, multi-ethnic city. So different from the little Italian village where I live. My friend Aasiya lives here, she is going to a wedding and asked me to go with her. I cannot miss this opportunity, so I accept enthusiastically. The day before the party, I realize I do not have a suitable frock for the occasion. I call her, "Hi Aasiya, I'm not going to the wedding, I don't have anything glittery for the evening".

On the other side of the receiver, her voice is soothing. "Since when is a dress a problem? I'll bring everything you need. Don't worry, see you tomorrow".

She hangs up on me, as usual she is in a hurry doing a million things.

I am left speechless, but I am soon amused by the idea of this unplanned adventure. On Saturday evening Aasiya arrives carrying a bag containing my wardrobe. I can choose between two *dirac*, matching *garbasaar, shash* and petticoat with a rich flouncy lace. A *parure* of twenty-four karat gold filigree necklace, bracelet and earrings. Also, she brings me a pair of stylish glittering Asian designer evening shoes to match. "Pity! They aren't my size."

I choose the pink *dirac* and its twin set. Aasiya works on my hair, she styles the *shash* in a turban fashion, letting my earrings show.

I do not interfere. She is in charge. I have a glance at myself in the mirror, it is like I am going back decades; for a few moments images of shiny golden bracelets, pale saffron rice, blinding white houses, deep purple bougainvillea bushes, the bright emerald sea come to me, like a skilful artist spattering colourful paint on a white canvas.

The voice of my friend, "It is the *moda* of Mogadishu when we were young," brings me back. I control my giggle.

The silk *garbasaar* covers my shoulder. I am standing in front of the full-size mirror and see this pink *confetto* woman staring back at me. I do not recognise myself. Aasiya hands me the pink lipstick to complete the masquerade.

She looks at me joyfully; I do not have the heart to disappoint her. A last look and I decide, "We're going to a wedding, not a funeral! Fine."

Deep in my heart I would not have the guts to go on a bus by myself dressed like this. Thank God, Aasiya has a car. Sitting comfortably in the vehicle she tells me, "We are going to pick up other ladies; they don't drive, so I am in demand," winking at me.

London boroughs are extensive; we have time and do not mind the slow and dense traffic of the weekend. We talk, laugh and sing along to *Azzurro* by her favourite Italian singer, Adriano Celentano. Aasiya remembers the time when she went to study in Italy in the late sixties. Those songs bring back lost nostalgic memories.

The car is bursting with music, perfume, giggles, the latest gossip and jokes; after finally picking up our last passenger, we arrive at the hotel. In the car park, I panic and start having doubts, "Maybe I am too dolled up, I look ridiculous with these colours."

I turn to my friend, our eyes meet; she is thrilled and striking in her sparkling blue dress. I gain courage and trot through the hall. The lounge is teeming with people. It has been a long time since I last saw so many Somalis in one place. I fill my eyes with the beauty of the scene.

We take seats at a round table for eight. Aasiya introduces me to the other guests. She knows many people, she is very popular. Guests continue to flow in; friends greet each other, loudly, hugging. Women do not meet often, because the distances in London are enormous, but they use the phone daily to pass the *sheeko sheeko*.

At the table a lot of mobile phones ring, voices whispering to the ones who could not come. Pictures are sent instantly to the corners of the world.

The younger generations are born and raised in Britain. The girls do not wear a headscarf. You can notice they have spent the whole morning at the hairdresser. They seem to come out of a fashion magazine. Straight silky hair and soft highlights frame big eyes; fake lashes, deep black *kajal* and full glossy lips.

Long slim necks come out of light, transparent rainbow coloured *dirac*. This unique Somali garment fully covers their body showing only the tip of the evening shoes. These young women prefer costume jewellery: huge bright stones adorning their fingers, long variegated beads twisted around their breast, dangling earrings, intricate bracelets.

The swarming voices and laughter rise above the music. Live Somali musicians start entertaining us. Men are sitting separately in the same hall; they are stylish too. Personalities from the Somali TV channel are the stars of the evening: journalists, anchormen, they mingle with the crowd.

The music changes; the bride and groom are coming. There is silence. All eyes are on the bride: she is wearing a long white wedding dress, her bare shoulders covered with tiny glittering diamonds. She is wearing a crown. It is a fairytale. They are gorgeous, holding hands, their hearts beating fast, a smile full of promises. Like a king and a queen they take their seats on thrones.

Family and friends are longing to take the microphone and to recite the verses they have composed for the newlyweds. The audience claps and the poetry begins: the rhythm is intense, each verse praises the genealogical tree of the couple. It is a poetry competition. Everything is so frenetic, the intricate language carries our memories and imaginations to far lands, where footsteps of camels encounter clouds of frankincense and myrrh; the sounds of ancient lullabies, women chanting and hyenas dancing under the full moon.

The cameraman is moving around the guests, capturing every moment. Photo albums are no longer popular, now it is the era of the CD. All these images will go on Facebook and YouTube. They will be watched over and over again.

Dinner is served, photographic lens's slide on the food. I was looking forward to tasty Somali cooking. White waiters serve Middle Eastern appetisers, garnished on pretty plates: olives, humus, couscous, *baba-gannoush* and *falafel*. Our taste buds travel around the planet. Exotic fruit punch is served in long transparent glasses with silly little umbrellas.

The final touch is a rich multi-layered cake for the bride and groom to cut together and share hilariously. A cup of crème caramel is brought to our table. I did not give up, I was still expecting *xalwo*, a cake made of ghee, sugar, rose water and spices that never came, and *gahwo*, but it was an ordinary Nescafè.

People started swaying; revival songs were pulling even the shyest to the dance floor. A tribute to Michel Jackson took us on a moon walk. Then the latest music was playing and I was lost. The young people were in a delirium. The old and new were mixing; life goes on.

You could feel mothers, deep in their hearts, wishing for a good husband for their daughters. A happy lasting marriage. Nowadays young couples want an extravagant and expensive wedding. It is a way to show off who had the best party. Families are buried in debts. Husband and wife, as soon as they encounter incomprehension, separate. May Allah protect our loved ones.

The Shop

I am walking along the Coventry Road, I love the atmosphere. All around me: shops, supermarkets selling everything from cutlery to plastic flowers, items you do not find in Marks & Spencer. Everything has this style that does not go out of fashion; it is as if time has frozen. You can find the same tea cups with the golden ring of twenty years ago, the bright plastic water jugs, and people who still buy them.

The *halal* butcher's shop is not the place for people who shop in the fresh food departments for little packages of meat that has lost its original shape. Here the whole animal is on display: legs, head, liver, heart, tripe. The smell gets into your nostrils, and if you are not used to it you can feel uncomfortable.

The sweet shops have mountains of *baklava*, rich with almonds, pistachio, walnuts, spices and honey that make your mouth water.

The fruit and vegetables stalls take you to faraway countries: bananas of every size, juicy plump mangoes, pineapples with yellow and green smiling faces, coconuts that makes you dream of long white beaches, and pungent red chilies, each one bringing stories from remote villages.

The fast-food shops are replicas of the big chains but have a different flavour: masala, kebab, naan, pitta, hommous and *bajiyas*.

Bakeries sell several different kinds of Arabic bread, side by side with doughnuts.

In the Islamic bookshops you are intrigued by the variety of books and audio-visual material in English that deals with different ethic and religious matters, from children's education to Islamic law, from history to biographies of the most important figures of Islamic culture.

Some barber shops have Somali names like *Benadir, Hamar Adde, Shangani*.

Banks with Asian signs, currency exchanges, international phone cards on special offer: by spending a few pennies you can reach far away friends.

An old church converted into a mosque. Schools, signs offering English and Arabic courses or computer training or preparing people to get British citizenship.

The whole street is alive with people, young dads with beards and skull caps pushing buggies.

College students in *niqab*. Women wearing headscarves. Elderly Somali men wearing the typical embroidered cotton hat and cosy shawls. You can spot their thick red, henna-dyed beards from afar.

Many mixed couples, men with blue eyes and red hair, wearing *thobes* and leather jackets. The new Muslim generation. I like the style and the creativity of their Islamic urban look. Warm woollen material, soft colours, they match the damp autumn. *Kefia* and *kofias* complete their style. They are functional, dynamic; they belong to this vibrant city. They are not icons from desert lands.

I arrive at the Salaama Shopping Centre, a two-storey building. On the first floor there are mainly offices. On the ground floor, a cafeteria, a tailor, a bureau de change and many small shops owned by women.

It is late in the morning and many premises are still closed. I find one that is opening. A lady is displaying skirts, *abayas* and dresses to attract clients.

My silent footsteps take her by surprise; she jumps, turns around and looks at me. She greets me, "*Assalamu aleikum.*"

"*Waaleikum salaam, iska warran*, how are you?"

She is astonished; her face opens with a wide smile, "*Abaayo Somali maa tahay?* Sister, are you Somali? I thought you were an Arab."

"I am Somali, born in Mogadishu."

"*Xaggee baad deggened?* Where did you live?"

"Bondere."

"*Soo dhawow*, welcome, come in, I am Fouzia."

"I am Naima, *barasho wanaagsan*, nice to meet you."

She looks motherly; her soft ample body is wrapped in a large brown *abaya*, her short nails are covered with almost-black henna; calm almond shaped chestnut eyes are looking at me from behind a pair of modern spectacles.

The language of my hometown and a familiar face take me back to the old Mogadishu, when the neighbours used to invite you into their homes.

The small shop is bursting with goods. Shelves full of merchandise wrapped in transparent cellophane, hangers with long evening *abayas*, rigorously black, embellished with shining beads in the shape of gigantic fantastic flowers. Colourful rayon and cotton skirts, long inviting dresses, fancy plastic and fabric handbags scattered on the floor, tiny elegant evening bags, simple headscarves in leopard-print.

In the glass showcase the perfumes are in miniature bottles decorated in gold: they contain oils of plants, flowers and bark from the Far East.

Creamy body lotion smelling of cardamom and cinnamon, air fresheners that take you to the Himalayan hills along roads and dusty trails.

Black seed oil and turmeric face scrub in decorative jars promise lovely young fair skin. Henna and hair dyes that can conceal rebellious grey. In here, everything belongs to a woman's world.

Glittering gold-plated jewellery and fake precious stones catch my eyes.

In a corner piles of acrylic blankets, heavy bedspreads and curtains.

Two authentic Somali leather *ghember* and the everlasting handmade limestone incense burner give personality to the setting.

There are also modern electrical burners of different sizes.

I am scanning everything, many items are packed and stuffed under the shelves.

Fouzia invites me to sit on an old swivel office chair, and I do so automatically.

She moves around the shop, I notice she is limping slightly. Maybe arthritis, or a bullet from the war, I do not dare to ask her.

She slips a CD into a small hi-fi, adjusts the volume and a serene masculine voice fills the room, reciting *suras* from the Quran. Fouzia lights a ball of charcoal and pops it in the burner, and then she throws in a pinch of *luuban*. Rich, intense clouds of frankincense dance towards the ceiling and blend with the other aromas.

I imagine that she performs the same gestures everyday.

"How come the other shops are closed?"

"They open late, there's not much business to be done in this season," she replies, sitting on a *ghember*.

"Do you live far from here?"

"Yes, I have to take two buses, but I like to come early and stay until seven in the evening."

"Looking at the shop windows, I've noticed that all of you have more or less the same items. How come?"

"Once it was difficult to find *abayas*, long dresses, *dirac*, so women started to open shops. Now there are too many of us!"

Then, pointing at the large thermos, she asks me:

"Are you having tea or coffee?" She opens a container and adds, "I prepare *samosas* and *buur* in the morning, bring them here for the ladies who want to have breakfast. It costs one and a half shillings."

She laughs, for a moment she looks younger.

"It's one pound fifty, but I like to express myself in shillings".

I smile, and the shilling takes us back to Mogadishu.

"Is it *gahwo* or Nescafè?"

"*Gahwo iyo sanjabil waie.*"

"I'll have *gahwo* with two *samosas*; I don't fancy *buur*."

She hands me the boiling cup, the aroma of ginger makes me feel good. The *samosas* are homemade; they are big, thick and have irregular shapes, not like those perfect tiny machine-made ones. The meat filling is rich and spicy, you can taste the onion.

I am relaxed and enjoy my snack.

A bubbly woman in a black *abaya* enters, greeting us in a cheerful voice. She grabs a short stool and sits down. You can tell that she is not a guest here.

She studies me with her piercing eyes and is eager to know more about me, "Do you live in this area? I've never seen you before."

"I'm visiting from Italy".

"Italy? Where in Italy? I was in Turin for a short time and I didn't like it at all!"

"Why didn't you like Turin?"

"People give you bad looks over there. They're very distrustful towards Muslims. I stayed at my cousin's house for one month. They'd like to leave the country, but their children grew up in Italy and are reluctant to move".

"I like it here, you can dress up as you please, nobody bothers you," and I go on, "Fouzia, your *samosas* are superb. Next time I come to this part of town, I'll definitely come to visit you."

"Come whenever you like, you're always welcome."

I pay my shilling and a half, hug my home girls and leave.

The cold air outside reminds me that I am very far from Mogadishu, but the little time I have spent with those ladies revived the unique hospitality of my people.

Hamar Adde

The tiny council house is squeezed between many other identical buildings facing an old railway. I have not seen trains passing for ages. There are neither trees nor a flower pot along this road. It is as if a painter decided to paint these houses with no colour or life.

In reality, life is bubbling inside these homes. My friend Safia lives here with her seven children, in a house designed to accommodate a family of four. She is in line to be assigned a better house, but the list is long.

It is amazing the way she is coping with this situation. The thing that impressed me the first time I visited her is how tidy, pleasant and welcoming the place is.

Coming through the front door, you are directly in the living room. Ivory pastel colours make the room look wide; two light brown sofas, matching colourful cushions, a creamy carpet on the floor. Hanging from the walls are small decorative objects made of tiny golden, white and black beads: they give the house an oriental look. Arabic calligraphy reminding us that Allah protects the house. An old-fashioned television is sitting in the corner, very discreet, not like those huge invasive plasma screens that you now find even in modest houses. An electric heater inserted in a disused fireplace spoils the atmosphere. Draped embroidered curtains frame the window, a touch of elegance.

In the dining room a table that has seen better times, folding chairs coated in steel with padding on the seats and backs in a vivid red plastic material, a bookshelf, a small television. The room is bright and a modern clock is ticking on the wall. The flooring is laminated; it is easy to clean. In this space the children study, eat, play and watch their favourite shows.

The kitchen looks more like a corridor; it is narrow. The sink, the cupboards, the washing machine and the cooker are wedged together, allowing only one person to stand still while cooking. Safia can move with her eyes closed; she knows every inch of it by heart. Here she prepares the best tasty food for her big family. Shopping for eight people can be a nightmare, but I guess it is all about how you train yourself.

She is a strong brave Somali woman who left her country because of the war. She is divorced; her husband left her for a fresh catch. She got a driving licence, bought a car and moves in the heavy traffic to meet the busy schedule of her kids.

The firstborn is starting college, while the last one is two years old.

Safia is a daydreamer with one foot on the ground; she is in her late thirties and has a lot of energy. Her ambition to become a nurse takes up most of her time and energy: at the moment she is taking classes to improve her English; she knows that one day she is going to make it.

Her wish and great hope is to move from this neighbourhood. The windows of her car have been smashed, the body scratched several times. When she goes out of the house, there is always a bunch of teenagers sitting on the bonnet of her car, but she keeps quiet. They look scary: tattoos, skinheads, piercing's, leather jackets, mini-skirts, high heels, dyed hair, heavy makeup, long nails painted with flashy nail polish. With fags between their fingers, they give her nasty looks; she does not open her mouth to say one word. Safia does not look for trouble. Several times the police have come to her neighbours' houses. They drink, fight and make a lot of noise. In the morning beer cans and broken bottles are on her doorstep.

She bears it all. She wants to set a good example for her children, but is conscious that she cannot keep them wrapped in cotton wool. After school she takes them to the *madrasa*, to read, write and recite the Quran and understand its values.

Safia speaks to her children in Somali, because she wants them to learn their mother tongue. In fact, apart from the eldest, the others are born and bred in the United Kingdom. The younger ones, when they speak to each other, use English. I like to hear their broken *af-somaali* with a strong British accent.

Once, I was reading a book with them; it was about some children at the beach, so I asked, "Have you been to the seaside?"

"No, but we go to the swimming pool," answered Samia with a clever look.

"*Hooyo* promised she will take us to Somalia," remarked Farhan.

I was looking at their beautiful faces, realising that they have never been out of this city.

"What do you imagine Somalia is like?" I asked.

For a moment there was silence, eyes wide open; then Hussein, who is in year two, raised his arms and said, "Big buildings."

"Lions walking in the street," roared his twin brother, Hassan.

"But a lion can eat the people if it is hungry," stated Omar.

I wish I could say, "*Abracadabra!*" and have the magic wand to take them to *Hamar Adde*, the fairy tale land of my childhood.

I did not know which Somalia to describe, the past or the present?

I wanted to protect them from the image of this war-torn country, from the horrors of the famine that is killing livestock, children and old people.

I was grasping at places, images where the beauty is still intact.

I started telling them. "Do you know that Somalia has endless white sand beaches? That children in Mogadishu learn to swim in the big waves of the Indian Ocean? You do not need to wear jumpers or coats or wellies. The sun always sets at the same time and the nights are long. The moon is so bright that you can see without the street lights."

Staring at their expressions, I said, "Do you know, there are huge elephants? ...Who knows how to say elephant in *af-somali*?"

They were silent...

"*Ma roo di...*" I sounded out, and we were all saying it, louder and louder, *maroodi, maroodi...* laughing!

"There are ancient mosques and little alleys with no names in the old town.

The donkeys are so beautiful, they have long ears, big sweet eyes and long lashes; on their short strong legs they walk all day, carrying water tanks to the houses. The sky is always blue..."

I would have carried on forever, but children need to see, to touch, to smell and to remember.

Eid Al-Adha

I am very glad to celebrate *Eid* in Birmingham, a city that reminds me of my hometown, Mogadishu. Not architecturally, but in its multiculturalism. I grew up hearing the sound of different languages around me. I felt a sense of security walking through narrow alleys and busy streets. The twin bell towers of the cathedral stood majestically next to minarets of ancient coral stone mosques. The sound of the bells shattered the moving clouds, while the noble voice of the muezzin deeply touched the hearts of the believers.

Living in Italy, I missed the atmosphere of tolerance and respect. Our *Eid* would taste of anxiety, we would think, "Let's hope the council will give us the space for prayer, we have presented all the papers on time".

It is Sunday morning in Birmingham, the traffic flows lazily in the streets. I can spot some people walking along the way. Men wearing white *thobe* and *kofi*, women draped in their long dresses, walking briskly. It is cold. They too are heading to the mosque. The taxi drops us at the entrance.

The mosque is full of worshippers. We are greeted by their voices praising God on this blessed day, "*Allahu Akbar, Allahu Akbar.*"

I am with my beloved daughter and my grandson. He is wearing a creamy *thobe* and a knitted blue and beige skullcap; he looks gorgeous. We sit on the fleecy green carpet, joining the choir. Women of all ages keep on coming. A new mum is proudly carrying her newborn baby girl, like a pink wad of cotton. Weeping children are clinging to their mother's breast. Attractive young girls with colourful headscarves stand like flamingos in a pond. Fair-skinned bodies in their typical embroidered Moroccan kaftans cross their legs elegantly. Slim figures covered in black silk *abayas* with bright beaded *tusbih* whisper supplications. Graceful little girls with glittering dresses show off their henna tattooed hands. Expressive eyes are immersed in the reading of verses from the Quran. Humanity keeps on pouring in; we squeeze up trying to make room for them. Next to me a sister is wearing a turquoise scarf, enhancing her blue eyes. Her teenager daughter is looking at herself in a hand mirror, adjusting her flowered pin. In front of me is a large Somali family, the grandmother praising Allah loudly and bottle-feeding a plump chocolate infant. Next to me, on the right-hand side, a lady in her gold and red striped *sharwal-khamiz* is hushing her twin boys. Curious little eyes glancing at each other. They are all so pretty with their new clothes and stylish haircuts. Butterfly and flower-shaped pins hold long and short hair.

The imam announces that the prayer is to begin. We all stand in a straight row, shoulder to shoulder. There is an eloquent silence. The toddlers are left sitting on the floor. The babies are lying on the carpet, wrapped in their soft blankets, only their little hands and legs are moving. The older children are standing, ready to pray. The full-bodied voice of the imam leads the congregation. We all raise our hands in supplication, recite the *Fatiha*, then we bow till our forehead touches the floor. I feel my fragility as a human being in front of my Creator. I could bow there forever and never be thankful enough for all the blessings He has bestowed on me. The verses of the Quran bring tears to my eyes. We end the prayer saying, "*Assalamu Aleikum wa Rahmatullahi*," turning our face first to the right and then to the left.

Joy is floating in the air. We greet each other saying, "Happy Eid." I hug and kiss women I have never met and that, probably, I will never meet again. I feel the humanity, the sisterhood; there is no pride of wealth and beauty.

Polite smiling ladies are offering chocolates, toffees and dates from rectangular boxes. Homemade cupcakes, fig rolls and baklavas are quick to go. We all leave the mosque to let another group in. They have been waiting at the main entrance for the next session of prayers.

Everything is so well-organized. We use the back door to leave after putting on our shoes which were carried, up to this moment, in little blue plastic bags provided by the *masjid*.

The sun is glowing; it is a bright, chilly day. Men wearing different styles of Islamic hats are coming out of another door. Well-groomed long silver-white beards distinguish older men holding their inseparable *tusbih*. Wrinkled and smooth-skinned fingers pushing malachite, tiger eye and sandalwood beads, automatically, while searching for their wives, offspring, sisters, mothers, aunties, cousins and grannies. Small circles of friends and relatives stand hugging, chatting and sprinkling cheerfulness around the crowd. We come across a few acquaintances and greet each other in high spirits. I can feel the festivity. I count ten different languages spoken in this gathering. Cars are filled with noisy passengers waving hands from the windows; many others walk calmly towards the bus stops.

Restaurants, coffee shops, sweet shops and bakeries are starting to open. We are heading to an area set up for entertaining kids. Excited children jumping and rolling on a bouncy castle, or sliding hilariously. Little ones riding on horses, in police cars, on buses on a merry-go-round. The ride does not last long and the children want more. One pound, nowadays, is worth little. Stalls selling pink and white candy floss, popcorn, sweets. We have had enough. We stroll to a peaceful nearby park. Meadowland and rows of big leafy trees, shy squirrels hiding behind branches, bloated pigeons feeding on the remains of crisps, pizza and bread that people did not bother to throw in a bin. My grandson is full of energy. He is on the monkey bars. His mum is looking after him. Other children are playing on the swings and climbing wall. I sit on a nearby bench; the sun is warming my shoulders. I am looking at my grandson; he is happy. He is having fun. We told him that this is a special day. The day Prophet Ibrahim was ordered by the Lord to sacrifice his son. When the Prophet told his son, "Ismail, I had a dream last night. Allah wants me to sacrifice you," Ismail was not afraid. He loved Allah very much and knew Allah never does anything to harm people. Ismail laid down on the ground. He closed his eyes. His father picked up the knife. Ibrahim was ready to obey Allah to sacrifice his son. At that moment the angel Jibril appeared with a ram to be sacrificed instead. They thanked Allah and then the Prophet sacrificed the ram. Allah commanded the believers to observe this day as *Eid Al-Adha* or the Feast of Sacrifice.

I remember *Eid* when I was a child growing up in Mogadishu. We do not have all these amusements, parks and bouncy castles. *Eid* is celebrated mostly at home with families, friends and neighbours.

There is always talk about some relatives who went to *Hajj* and how lucky they were to experience *Eid* in the Holy land.

Early in the morning, after the *Eid* prayer, men scented with musk and amber and dressed in their traditional clothes come out of the mosque chanting, "*Allahu Akbar, Allahu Akbar.*"

The gate of our house is open and I can hear people entering and greeting one another, "*Assalamu Aleikum.*"

Men are directed to the room reserved for them. Women are cooking in the garden; the kitchen is not big enough. The smell of spicy lamb wafts from huge aluminium pots, gathering hungry tabby cats with big dark-rimmed eyes. They wait for their share in the shadow of frangipani trees. Trays full of glasses filled with red syrup and lime juice, cold thanks to the ice cubes swimming in them, are available to all the guests. Homemade biscuits prepared the night before are piled on large decorated trays produced in China. They are my favourite, crumbly and fragrant. The taste of ghee, cardamom, cinnamon and brown sugar is unforgettable. The starters: liver cooked in sliced red onion, cumin and green chilli, hearty crispy *samosas*; tripe simmered in spices and cherry tomatoes until it melts in the mouth, savoury lentil and oxen soups. Boys with long legs like ostriches are ready to serve from heavy dishes of yellow saffron rice garnished with sultanas and caramelised onions, roasted meat, potatoes, fresh mixed green salads, tamarind sauce, coconut grated and crushed with lime chilli and garlic.

In the shade of the jacaranda tree two sweaty helpers are singing and washing glasses, jugs, plates and trays faster than a modern dishwasher. Lots of movement, children chasing each other, shabby aunties holding greasy wooden spoons as a weapon, screaming, "Stop running!"

I was four or five years old, the first time I can remember I saw a lamb in our garden. I was amused. I thought it was to be my pet. My mum told me to stay away from the animal. I did not listen. I was touching its smooth skin, all white with brown patches, and playing with its silky floppy ears. The innocent watery eyes looking at me and the incessant bleating. I was bewitched by this gentle animal. Its agile legs would run a few steps from me and then stop, not afraid of me anymore. My lamb would eat from my hand, just like our cat.

At night I shut my eyes, hearing its bleat sneaking onto my pillow. The next morning I rushed into the garden: my lamb was not there!

The house was in full swing. A lot was going on for the preparation of *Eid* day. I did not realise that my lamb had been slaughtered.

Later I discovered that my lamb was transformed into the juicy chunks of meat that everybody was chewing. Joy and celebration around me. Even the beggars were delighted, scraping the last grain of rice from their bowls. I was hurt; I experienced a feeling I could not fully understand.

I grew up puzzled thinking about why we have to feel pain to experience joy. I am peeling potatoes while listening to an Islamic radio station; a scholar is explaining the meaning of *Eid Al-Adha*. He is saying, "Just imagine how we feel when we slaughter an animal that was with us only for a few hours. Think about the bonding, and how hard it is to sacrifice it. Now imagine how it felt for the Prophet Ibrahim, to obey at the command of Allah. It is a day to remember his devotion to God Almighty's Command, and how Allah is Merciful."

These key words gave a meaning to what I had in my heart for a long time. Knowing that this meat is going to be shared with the poor gives meaning to this sacrifice.

A tight little smile came on my face, remembering the receipt I kept in the pocket of my handbag. It is a donation I made to a charity just days before *Eid*. My conscience is at peace; I fulfilled my duty. In a faraway country, torn by war and famine, a child will taste, for the first time, the flavour of meat.

New Generations

Anisa has her eyes open in the semi-dark room. In this place the darkness of the night is not shrouded with the brightness of the moon and the stars. Street lights filter through the worn flowery cotton curtains. The silence of the night is ripped apart by the sound of a siren. She stretches her legs, tired of keeping them folded under the blanket. The house is quiet, her ears pricked, every second marked by the clock on the bedside table feels like ages to her distressed mind. Images of war flow: blood, wounded people, dead children, the face of her husband Ridwan killed by bandits in Mogadishu, the people of her neighbourhood disfigured by terror. She managed to leave the country with her four small children.

Eight long years have passed since that day. The English government took care of them: a house, welfare to support her kids, then British citizenship and, finally, a job for her. Anisa is a strong woman, she does not cry about her past, although her current situation as a school cleaner, mopping floors, is different from her life in Mogadishu.

She was an office clerk. Now she has to bring up her children with no relatives around. The only member of her family is her uncle, who lives in Melbourne, Australia. The women in her neighbourhood are strangers, they do not speak to one another; it is not like in her hometown, where they knew each other and used to share kitchen utensils, have tea, gossip, watch over the children, prepare food for weddings, exchange recipes, decorate their hands with *henna*, watch their favourite TV programmes together. Your neighbour became a member of your extended family. Now all that is gone. Her heart is full of grief for her eldest son, Aden.

She feels a pain in her chest that contracts her muscles and she opens her mouth, gasping for air. She is waiting for the main door to open, to hear silent footsteps walk in, like a burglar in the night. Only then can she sleep.

She no longer gets out of bed to ask him, "Aden do you know what time it is? Where have you been? Do you know how worried I was about you? Who were you with? What do you do at this time of night?"

Once she threatened to kick him out of the house. He did not show up for two days. She thought she was losing her mind…

Now there is silence between them.

"Who is this boy with the baggy jeans that slip off from his waist letting the elastic of his underwear show?"

"Who is this person, always wearing headphones, who does not speak to me, who comes home late at night and goes around with people I do not know?"

I do not recognise him anymore, my Aden, a piece of my heart.

"Who is this rebel, this surly boy that keeps moving through my house like a ghost?"

She tried to reason with him, talking to him gently. Once she slapped him; he told her, "Next time I will call the police."

In this country if you raise your hand to your children there is the risk of losing them. The government can take them away.

The world outside is prey to gangs who sell drugs, to paedophiles and death merchants.

The sound of a siren quickens her heartbeat.

"Why am I in this situation? Is it because Aden does not have a father?"

She remembers Ridwan's smooth dark face, his small sharp nose, like an eagle's, his piercing brown eyes, his short silky ebony hair covering his scalp; how brief was their life together!

A man who did not cause her big problems. He was stubborn; once he took a decision he would not change his mind, but she knew she could count on him. He took care of her; it was him who helped them escape from the war. He sent them to safety. He remained in Mogadishu, waiting for calm to return. He did not think the conflict would worsen. The news of his death reached her when they were safe in Nairobi.

"Nooo," thinks Anisa sadly, "it cannot be because Ridwan is dead."

It is this cursed war that eradicated us. We are numbers, we are labelled, we are refugees: Somali refugees. I know so many women that have husbands who are not present in their everyday life.

In the mornings I see groups of mothers taking children to school. I meet them everywhere, alone, doing shopping, at the parks, meeting the school teachers.

Men have become shadows. Their bodies weaken, sitting on carpets the whole night, drinking tea and chewing *khat*. Intoxicated by drugs they weave fanciful stories that look like the threads of a giant spider's web that slowly envelops their minds. In the daytime they sleep like bats hanging in a dark cave, eyes shut to the world around.

She could not have borne it if Ridwan had behaved like those men.

Her body is stiff, "Why has my Aden, my first born, my love, changed in this way?"

She clearly remembers the day the headmaster called her. Aden had had a fight with a boy in his class. She was so worried; once at home Aden looked at her, his eyes full of hatred, and with his fist up told her, "You Somalis are pirates and terrorists; this is how he insulted me."

I saw the pain in the eyes of my child. How could I explain we are people who want peace when the violence is still going on, and newspapers and television give negative news about Somalia?

Now Aden does not listen to me. He is a teenager. They talk about teenagers in this society as if they are a special species. Adolescence is considered a time of life when nasty behaviour is permissible.

I want to protect my son from drugs, gangs, alcohol. I have saved him from the hell of Mogadishu to give him a better future." Anisa's eyes have no tears.

The phone rings, two long endless sharp sounds break her thinking. She lifts up the receiver, "Halluu?"

The voice on the other side is metallic, "Are you Aden Ridwan Mumin's mother?"

"Who are you? Aden no here."

"This is the police. Are you his mother?"

"Yes!"

"Madam, I am sorry, but we have to inform you that Aden has been shot. You have to come to the City Hospital."

The receiver slips from her hand, her knees are shaking. It is like receiving a stab. Her cry is swallowed by the walls of an old flat, on the sixth floor of a cement tower.

My Friend in London

I am impatient, minutes seem eternal. Time is so tricky, clocks lie; it all depends on my emotions. Why is it that when I am happy time flies and, at other moments, time seems to be dragged by a lazy turtle?

In Italy I have dreamed about and planned to come to this event for months. Finally here I am, standing under the beautiful golden Dome. Many people would call it the Dome of the Rock.

I am looking at the crowd rushing in from the entrance. I am not in the Holy Land, but in the heart of the European capital of finance, London. The Islam Expo, Europe's biggest exhibition of modern day Islam. There is a lot going on: theatre, seminars, comedy, concerts, lectures, book launches, exhibitions, conferences; it is a four day event. My appointment is here.

Last night we spoke to each other and we decided: we'll meet at Al-Aqsa, we cannot miss each other. Not a word of which colour we would wear, or if we would carry a red umbrella, no signs. It is obvious; we cannot miss each other. We have been friends since we were at school.

Here she is, walking towards me, a tall, handsome young man at her side. We recognise each other simultaneously. We hug for a long time. Forty years roll back... cheerful girls, school uniforms and dreams cocooned in our peaceful city.

It is not easy to narrate what happened in all these decades. We laugh; I look at her son. I cannot believe she is a granny too, like me. We are the same age, we had different destinies.

I left the country many years ago...

She stayed, got married, had children, became a brilliant lawyer.

Twenty years ago the war broke out, her whole life turned upside down. She struggled; now she stands on her feet. She is a very important member of the Somali community. She opened one of the first *madrassa* for Somali children. She helped many refugees;

legally, she won cases where young Somalis would have been deported. She is always on the front line.

Today she was part of a group of lawyers who prepared the new constitution of the Somali Federal Government.

I remember what she told me between a smile and a serious face, "*Abaayo*, my dear sister, coming to Europe I am labelled a woman, a black woman, a Muslim woman, a refugee".

In Somalia she is a lawyer, a wife, a mother, a daughter, a sister, an aunt, a person!

Universal TV

Memories of my childhood in Mogadishu start with my dad turning on the radio early in the morning.

The house is full of music and voices speaking foreign languages. He prepares his shaving tools: safety razor, blades, soap, brush, bowl, a small jug of water and a face-towel. I love watching him, looking like Father Christmas, only his big hazel eyes smiling at me, peeping above that coat of white foam. He is whistling the tunes; we smile. Looking at him I know he is the best dad in the world. As soon as the radio announces that the BBC news is starting, the mood changes: it is silence, I have to freeze!

This serious, emotionless male voice fills the air. I do not have any idea where London is, except that it is in a far and very important land.

Now we live in the satellite era everything is so different.

Universal TV is a product of its time. Most of the world population would say, "Universal TV? Never heard of it, what is it?"

It is not CNN, Fox or Al-Jazeera, although its popularity is rapidly growing in these recent years, like an oil spill, in the five continents.

It is a TV satellite channel in Somali. It is the most important channel for information on Somalia, a country that has been forgotten by the world media. It unites the Somali Diaspora, scattered in every corner of the planet.

Inspired by Raghe Omar, the famous British-Somali journalist, young, talented female and male correspondents give news from Mogadishu, London, Cairo, Cape Town, Rome, Hargheisa, Sana'a, Amsterdam, Oslo, Lusaka and many other cities.

There are people who choose not to watch this channel. They want to avoid the crude scenes of death and violence captured everyday in Mogadishu. There is no image censorship; the reality is transmitted without filtering or cuts. A western viewer would not understand.

We, in the West, are used to seeing war from screens that show us phosphorescent dots where intelligent bombs and precise drones make people and buildings disappear like magic. There is no blood, no mutilated limbs, no sound of people suffering, no screaming, no desperation. It is a virtual war; it is clean, like the one kids amuse themselves with on the latest Play Station.

The eye of Universal TV takes us crudely to our reality, our truth. It is the technological umbilical cord that unites us with the wound that has never healed, with a country that is in a limbo where peacekeeping forces, to maintain peace, slaughter innocent people.

Talk shows give viewers who are scattered around the world, hopeless and wounded, the opportunity to say what they think about and wish for their motherland. Many times it has been said to the privileged western Somali refugees that, from their cosy existence, they do not understand and have no right to interfere in the politics of the nation.

Is it a sin to have saved one's life and the life of one's loved ones from the horrors of war?

Who sends money and always takes care of the ones left behind?

Who, if not the exiled?

Young and old people take part in these discussions in a very civilised manner.

On Fridays, an important day of the week in Islam, religious programmes and humanitarian appeals touch the hearts of believers. Money is collected to buy food for the needy, to drill water holes, to build basic clinics, to ship medicine, blankets, wheelchairs, milk powder and mosquito nets for preventing malaria, second-hand clothes and all that could alleviate the suffering of people who are deprived of a basic infrastructure.

The diaspora is united without any clan differences to help their fellow brothers and sisters in need.

When four-year-old Bilal watched the cartoons, he said, "Mum, where did Tom and Jerry learn to speak Somali?"

He was amazed. I loved watching *The Lion King* on the small screen, speaking with different Somali accents and dialects.

Somalis are good and imaginative; the latest Turkish and Gulf soap operas are dubbed in *af-Somali* and so are the popular Bollywood movies.

Sheeko Gaaban, the authentic, genuine short stories shot in Mogadishu, have poor quality images. The scenes are shot indoors; it is too dangerous outside. The actors are always the same ones, loved by the viewers; the message is direct and spontaneous, often accompanied by sarcasm and black humour.

Across the continents families announce weddings and newborns, and they send messages of happiness and congratulations to their extended families.

The music programme is on demand, with the latest videos. Classical and romantic Somali music melts the hearts of lovers.

Lately famous artists have come together to compose patriotic songs, trying to reinforce the general commitment to peace and unity. Among the younger generation music is changing; the culture is mixing, reflecting their having been brought up in foreign countries, from Australia to Norway.

Sport events that take place in Somali communities around the world give pride to young athletes.

Chefs compete and share their latest recipes on fancy programmes.

The most dramatic news is followed by a TV commercial.

We are immersed in a glossy, tempting world: the promise of a secure investment, even after the financial crisis in proprieties in Dubai, showing luxurious apartments for sale in modern skyscrapers. Villas with swimming pools immersed in lush palm groves, fragrant frangipani flowers and giant baobab trees in Kenya, where the Indian Ocean laps the East African coast, are the dream of the ones who want to get away from the grey and cold weather. Patented Somali brands guarantee the quality of herbal creams: they promise to rejuvenate and whiten the skin. Jewellery shops in the gold market in Dubai display the must-have items for a bride: necklaces, rings, bracelets, earrings, belts of filigree, pearls and diamonds. The textile emporium sells the latest silk, cotton, rayon and satin designs for *dirac* and *abayas*; the Somali woman, from the Middle East to the European capitals, creates her *moda*. Oriental perfumes, *oud, attar*; ready-made kits for applying *henna* transform hands into works of art, giving women the final, most extravagant, feminine touch. Phone cards with musical names advertise the cheapest rate for long-distance calls. Money transfer and money exchange bureaus offer the latest service: with a text message they can reach clients in remote destinations. Money leaves cities like London to reach a camel driver on the banks of the river Juba.

The world is globalised, even if the only two currencies accepted everywhere are dollars and euros.

Text Messages

My mind travels fast every morning, even before my eyes open. My hand automatically grabs my mobile phone on the bedside table. My fingers type all the words I wish I could say with my voice while looking at my loved ones.

"Good morning, my darling, hope you all had a good night's sleep. I will call you in the evening. I am so sorry that we are not there for Nabila's birthday. I remember your first birthday, as if it were today. Mum x"

Today is my granddaughter's birthday; I feel bad I am not with her to celebrate. I was with my family during the Christmas holidays. I bought Nabila a sleeveless light green velvet dress, pleated at the waist, with lots of tiny purple, yellow and blue flowers, and a cream jumper to go with it. She was very happy when I gave it to her and she told me with her cheeky face, "I will wear it for my birthday, so all my friends *saranno spiazzate*."

She will be six and has a clear mind about what to wear and which colours to put together. You cannot convince her if she does not like something. I was very glad I found her style.

My legs are stiff; I am not young any more and I need time before jumping out of my warm, cosy bed. My thoughts go to my daughter and her two children in Italy. She is one hour ahead of Birmingham. She is on her way to work. She commutes; the road is full of traffic, lorries, cars. I can see her itinerary.

Every morning we write to each other. We are so connected that, often, our text messages arrive simultaneously. For me, to read those few words is a blessing. "Good morning *Juma Mubarak* - I was texting you and your message arrived. We all had a good night's sleep apart from Taha who had a nightmare and woke up screaming. I held him in my arms and in two seconds he was snoring. *Inshallah* that we are always in good health. Lots of love. I feel sleepy!"

"It is very cold this morning, I just parked my car, arrived at the office, love."

These short messages full of life give me the strength to cope with the pain of separation our family is facing at this time of our lives.

I know it is a great opportunity for my two grandchildren to visit us often in Birmingham. When I speak daily on the phone with them the youngest, who is three, says, "*Nonna*, I want to come to Birmingham, look!" he tells me, thinking I can see him.

My daughter tells me he is pointing at his suitcase, ready for departure. Nabila too wants to travel and visit her favourite places: The Thinktank Museum, The Sea Life Centre and the Botanical Gardens.

I take them to the Central Library, where they can swim in books and take part in many activities with other children.

If we were all living in Italy they could not experience this, so in life we should accept both the sweet and the sour.

I feel I am living a double life: one is the reality of my everyday routine, which I am grateful to have and enjoy: preparing breakfast for my other grandchild, taking him to school, witnessing unique moments of him growing up. Taking him to the park and to the library, bathing him, holding his hand. Laughing and putting him right when he attempts to boss me around.

I am trying to balance my everyday journey of touch, smell and sight with the other world that I cannot touch or smell or see. My brain is split into two. I jump on the other track and see my daughter while she is cooking and shouting at her kids while we are on the phone.

I know her mood from the early morning, through the few words that appear on the tiny display of my mobile phone. We share condensed moments, when we caress or tease each other. In the early afternoon, on her way back home, I call her and we have those few minutes all by ourselves; she is calm, driving and with no kids around. We talk about our day.

This other far away world is so real that it is interwoven into the world that I am physically living in. Small things, like the sight of a mother climbing onto the bus with her toddler in a buggy, bring back images of my grandson smiling at me when we travelled together.

PART EIGHT

The Village

I am new to this village, as are the terraced houses painted in vivid orange and yellow colours, the playground with a red slide, swings, and a few wooden benches around it. The road is new, the streetlamps, the road signs, the tiny planted trees, everything is new. Even the chapel with Baby Jesus in the arms of his mother Mary is new; in contrast, the old houses cling together, and the long standing bell tower that chimes by the hour stands in remembrance of the partisans who died in the Second World War. The paint is long washed away from the building that was once a primary school.

I am walking towards the *piazza*, on the main street. Someone is peeping at me through white lace curtains in windows decorated with flourishing red geraniums. I am going to the only grocery, where there is life in this sleeping village. While I enter, the smell of *parmigiano, fontina, provolone, salame, prosciutto, mortadella* and the sweat of people that have been stuck in the shop for ages, hit my nostrils. There is silence; I can feel the cold air and a few eyes staring at me.

"*Buongiorno*", I say. A short, stocky guy with a prominent belly is looking at me from behind the counter in his greasy overall. A baritone voice replies, "*Buongiorno, signora*". The sound of the slicing machine fills the air and he keeps on cutting.

He turns off the machine and says, "One hundred grams of *salame, signora* Renata. Anything else?"

"Four *rosette*".

She pays and leaves.

I wait for my turn.

The elderly lady before me, enveloped in her flowered sleeveless cotton pinafore and flip-flops, keeps talking about the late Giovanni, whose funeral was yesterday.

Bepi knows everything: funerals, baptisms, weddings, confirmations, who received communion, the inhabitants who have lived in the village for the past forty years ... He knows even more about their lives. It is the focal point of gossip: who lost their job, if a wife is cheating on her husband, who bought a new car, who has cancer. There are no secrets. The residents of the new area are whetting his appetite to gulp down more.

When there are no customers, he stands outside with crossed arms and looks at the cars passing. He soon loses hope in getting new clients. The families that have moved to the village recently prefer shopping in supermarkets, where "buy two get one free" offers are tempting.

It is my turn. Bepi, with a fake smile stamped on his face and eyes that want to dig into my deepest secrets, says, "Tell me *signora*, what would you like?"

"May I have six *rosette*, please?"

He puts the bread in a brown paper bag, weighs it, sticks on the price and asks me, "… Anything else?"

"That's fine. How much is it?"

His face has lost the smile and the sweaty skin turns pink.

"One euro eighty".

I pay and leave the *drogheria* saying "*Arrivederci*".

There is no reply and I walk out to breathe fresh air again, in the empty street.

A balding old man, with large braces holding up his baggy trousers, brushes past my shoulder. I greet him, "*Buongiorno*".

He walks straight ahead. A worn-faced woman, carrying a bunch of daisies in the front basket of her bike, going to the nearby cemetery, is pedaling calmly. I try to catch her eyes and greet her with a loud voice, "*Buongiorno*".

She passes by. The sun is at its zenith, birds are chirping and a lazy dog is yawning when I pass by its gate.

I feel numb to all my surroundings; the bright day, the delicate white butterfly circling, the green and grey lizards swivelling their eyes before running away and hiding under hot stones. A line of tiny black ants moving fast on a wall, a blade of grass growing from a crack in the asphalt. An angry wasp is looking for trouble. I am blind; there is an invisible hand that is squeezing my heart. I take a deep breath, I am a stranger again. I know I have to start all over again.

Suddenly, my memory takes me back.

Autumn, nineteen seventy-one; I have just arrived in Italy. I am greeted by a sun that does not warm me and trees that change colours before they lose their leaves. I can feel the cold in my bones, too much to bear for a girl born under an endless blue sky, in a city caressed by the Indian Ocean. A heavy long coat covers my whole body. Underneath I am wearing velvet trousers, a woollen vest and two jumpers, a long scarf made of some foreign wool, brown leather gloves, thick socks and boots. The white fur hat makes me look like an Eskimo from another planet. The cold is still with me. I bought my outfit from Upim, a huge popular store. My favourite department is the clothing. With Lucio Battisti singing romantic songs in my ears, I touch soft pullovers, roll-neck jumpers, coarse jeans and smart outfits. I read the prices, knowing that no sales assistant will come to bother me. I have decided that the fancy shops are not for me. Once I went in, duped by a smile and seduced into trying on clothes that did not attract me. Elegant short skirts, dolls dresses. I am in the changing room, trying them on, half naked; I am in a cold sweat and my head is spinning.

The lady does not give me time to look at myself in the mirror. She jumps inside the tiny closet, bombards me with compliments, "It looks so nice on you; it brings out your figure and, with your complexion, it's just perfect". This woman, with her full make-up, high heels, tight knee-length skirt, a cream sweater and pearls hanging from her neck, is trying to transform me into her image. I miss going to the Tamarind *souk* filled with the sounds of hooting Vespas, cawing crows and the buzz of talkative people. I miss going to the Indian and Arabic shops, to choose light cotton materials, dyed using pigments that give them sunny colours, as if stolen from tropical gardens. I miss my tailor Aydarous. We used to create dresses that would cover my legs. At last, I leave the boutique buying a sweater, which I was not convinced about but "It looks so nice on me because of my complexion".

The only thing I am really convinced about is that it cost me an arm and a leg.

In this climate I suffer from headaches, due to the habit of clenching my jaw and stiffening my muscles. I suffer from a psychological seasonal cold that does not abandon me. I developed cervical arthritis, a disease whose existence, only a few months back, I ignored. In this country people in the GP's waiting room talk about arthritis, bronchitis, coughs, blocked noses, tonsillitis, pneumonia and influenza with exotic names.

The chilly wind brings tears to my eyes. I am pushing my daughter's brand new buggy. She loves the cold and never misses her stroll in the park. Malaika is happy, and through her button-shaped ebony eyes she is embracing the world around her. The winter air does not scratch her, only her round cheeks change colour. They are red, like juicy apples.

By now, I think I know the city and my adventurous mood takes me to explore new places. I walk and walk along narrow streets, where there were once horse-drawn carriages. I pass a small *piazza* where a man wraps roasted chestnuts in paper bags, reminding me of the corn on the cob sold on the street corners of my hometown. In the park strong elm trees stand like guardians of a sanctuary; the only sound is the footsteps of hurrying passers-by, trampling on dead leaves, bicycles ringing bells. The ruins of an old medieval castle show its past glory.

I take an unfamiliar alley and realize I am confused, I do not know where I am. I panic; I am too scared to ask for directions. My husband's words still echo in my ears, "Only ask the *vigili* for directions".

My eyes search for men in uniform, but they meet only pale, tired faces staring at us. Minutes feel like hours, the roads are dark now. The shop windows and the street lamps light up, a thin fog is settling. Hot tears roll down my face; I cannot control them. My sight is blurring, I look at the buggy. The little round head, protected by a red bonnet, gives me courage. I am not alone; my sweet angel is with me.

Briskly I turn right, and finally I see the bright sign of Upim.

These memories bring strength to me; I put my chin up and walk towards my new house. I live in the countryside and, finally, have my own garden. My luxurious fence of white, pink, red and salmon oleanders, the fragrance coming from the bush of tiny jasmine flowers fill our summer nights. Short brown hairy trunks of palm trees with large green fan-shaped leaves warm my heart.

Time is passing, the balconies of the neighbourhood are decorated with giant wooden storks holding a bundle, pink or blue ribbons tied at the gates.

Our family too is blessed with grandchildren. We go to the playground, their small hands holding on to the swing chains, legs flying in the air, laughter spreading in the clouds.

I know people from my neighbourhood by name. They know me too. I have roots, I am a grandmother. I am here to stay.

It is a dark and gloomy November. I can see trembling lights on the window sills, I try to look more closely: pumpkin faces. It's Halloween. I am surprised; in this little village I was not expecting people to celebrate Halloween. Many years ago, I was in Manhattan, in Greenwich Village, when I first saw the huge allegorical wagons, skeletons, witches and monsters parading.

"Italy is changing," I think. "It is adopting new traditions."

In the evening, a doorbell rings and little voices scream, "*Dolcetto o scherzetto?* Trick or treat?"

Cheerful eyes behind Dracula and scary grotesque masks; smooth-skinned hands grab sweets to run off quickly. After midnight youngsters sing with tipsy voices. Faraway, the sounds of howling lonely dogs.

It is a chilly morning. I am strolling along the embankment. I am with my two-year-old grandchild, bundled warmly in his buggy. All around, frosted fields, emptiness, a stingy sun and silent birds circling in search of food. I feel a swift movement by my side, and a voice is shouting at me,

"Aisha! Where is *Maometto*, The Prophet?"

It is a man on a bicycle, a stranger. He is cycling fast; he turns and stares at us with a satanic sneer and a wild look.

I watch this figure as it disappears down the silent straight line of the ghostly path.

DNA

The *minestrone* is ready. The chicken breast with potato and rosemary will take a few more minutes to cook. My cousin Mulki is preparing dinner, the phone rings.

"Hello, *sided tahay*," she answers, recognizing her friend's voice.

"I'm very well, *waan ladanahay, e iska waran adigu*?"

"*Alhamdullilah*, I'm fine, always busy as usual."

"In this country we're always in a hurry, there's no time to enjoy life."

"How are the little ones doing?"

"*Alhamdullilah* they are fine, Fouzia has a bad cough, with this cold weather."

"*Aniga*, when the weather changes my knee hurts. It feels like sharp needles sticking into it; I've tried several medicines, but they don't help."

"We have to take it easy, what else can we do? If we were living in a tropical country, we wouldn't have problems with our bones."

"*Haa*, if we were in Africa, with that lovely hot sun getting into each pore of our skin. With this humid damp weather, you don't feel like setting foot out of the door."

"Have you heard from your mum and Anab? Are they doing fine?"

"Yes, they're good. I'm planning to go to see them in May. The tickets have gone up in price."

"But you told me you wanted your mum to come for a visit."

"At the *questura*, the police refused me the authorisation. They told me the best way is for me to travel to Ethiopia, to the Italian Embassy, and have a DNA test done. They want to be sure she is my mother before, maybe, getting the visa."

"Halima, this is madness! You're an Italian citizen and they treat you this way!"

"Yes, they don't care at all; they see my name and the dark skin. Swines!"

"How much is this test going to cost you?"

"Five hundred euros."

"Rip-off! How many years have passed since you last saw your mum?"

"I... I came to Italy when the civil war began in Mogadishu in 1991."

"It's nineteen years since you saw your *hooyo*?"

"What could I have done? Mum didn't want to leave the country, but then the situation deteriorated. *Hooyo* was in shock when she saw a cat with a mutilated human hand in its mouth running in the street. It was then that she decided to leave Mogadishu, with my sister."

"Halima, don't be sad, thank Allah she's not in a refugee camp in the middle of nowhere, that you can rent a house for them in Addis Ababa."

"Yes, you're right. I would have died if my family had been trapped in a refugee camp."

"*Inshallah*, Halima, soon you will see your mum!"

"*Inshallah*, you know she's never held my children on her lap. She's only seen photos. I'm not taking Fouzia and Haamid with me. I'm scared of diseases. You need so many vaccinations to travel overseas."

"Let's meet up for a fabulous lunch before you leave."

"Of course, we have to meet. The day of departure is so far; one Sunday I'll make you *samosas*."

"You always catch me by the stomach. Your cooking's delicious. Give a big kiss to the children."

"Same to you, say hello to Francesco from me."

"All right, *waan ismaqli doonaa*."

Mulki hangs up the phone and bitterness is growing inside her, like a tumour. She is thinking of her friend and that she is not the only one in this situation. So many people in Europe have big problems reuniting with their families; bureaucracy and new immigration laws create new difficulties every day.

Mulki told me that when she was on vacation in Kenya last year, she talked to a tall athletic German guy, travelling on his bike. Hans was a teacher who had left Heidelberg months before, crossed many countries and slept under a blanket of twinkling stars in African villages that had no names on the map. He shared maize porridge and goat stew with the locals. He met simple people, farmers, tailors, story-tellers, craftsmen; youthful and toothless elderly women, lots of gifted, noisy children, hungry to discover the world. He snatched moments of their everyday life.

In luxurious five-star hotels, buried in an oasis of lush green flora, he had the chance to show these photos to tourists and give lectures about his extraordinary journey. He made some money to pay for his travels.

Badante

The torrid Italian summer is unbearable; the windows are open, only letting hot air in the room. The voices of children playing downstairs are mingling with the noise coming from the television. The tiny brown dog on the neighbours' balcony is barking every time a child hits the ball against the wall of the cement yard. Not a tree to provide shadow. The four tall buildings form a square, creating an echo of sounds that float in the air.

Sardines deep-fried in oil, a rich tomato sauce with basil, *frittata* and the smell of coffee gushing from old *mokas* are not secrets kept in one's own kitchen; they cross the boundaries of these claustrophobic flats.

The one o'clock news catches her attention. She turns the volume up and is glued to the screen: a little boat overloaded with young men and a few women with babies has arrived on the shores of Lampedusa. The tone of the journalist is alarmed; Italy is being invaded by these helpless people.

Fortress Europe. No more people, we want only small numbers to enter, to work like dogs and go back when we do not need them any more. This is what Maryam is thinking, looking at her wrinkled hands after the anchorman moves to the weather. She loses her appetite.

Her back is aching. She has a slipped disc and she looks older than her age. She has worked for so many years and now can barely pay the rent of this studio flat. Now her job is mostly done by women coming from Eastern Europe. They work for less money and in the black market. And honestly, with all the media frenzy about immigrants, the natives prefer to give the jobs to whites. Black skin is not welcomed and it is always better not to bring an Islamist, a woman who wears a headscarf, into the house.

Maryam remembers when her hands were smooth and soft like caramel. She came to Italy from Somalia in the late seventies, looking for employment. At that time nobody was calling her *badante*, the new name given by the media to the health care workers who take care of the elderly. There were few women doing her profession and they mainly came from her country or from Eritrea.

Her hands combed locks of fragile silver hair hanging from bald scalps. She fed toothless jaws, spoon by spoon. She soaped and washed with care the geography of bodies that had lost the vigour of youth. Pampered delicate skin invaded by rigid veins carrying loads of rusted heavy scrap, like old rails running over skeletal arms.

All those women had names and now, one by one, they are gone. So many times the last stage is spent in an unfamiliar room of a big hospital, counting the few hours before their last breath.

As time went by, she learned how to cope with death. Her faith helped her: to Him we belong and to Him we shall return.

The Hijab

Nabila is following her mum like a shadow, nagging her with the same question: "*Mamma*, when are we going to get my scooter?"

Her mother is busy changing the bed sheets; Saturday is the only day of the week when she can tidy the house properly. During the week she has to commute and leave the house early in the morning to go to work. By the time she is back, after picking up Nabila from the nursery school and stopping at her parents' house where the little one spends his day, it is past five in the afternoon. Cook dinner, spend time with the kids, bath them and it is time to sleep. She remembers going to university, when her only job was to study. All her other needs were taken care of. She felt fortunate to have parents who were so loving and caring. Even now they are giving her a hand with her new family. Looking into the intelligent eyes of her daughter, she feels gratitude in her heart for being blessed with children.

Amina knows that her daughter deserves the push scooter, as she has done all the things she promised to do: clear up her playroom before going to bed, be nice to her younger brother, fold her clothes and keep her socks in pairs, not letting them disappear under sofas where it is difficult to find them. All this is not easy with Taha scattering toys around the house, taking mum and dad's shoes out of the shoe cupboard to wear them before hiding them. He plays with pots and pans making a lot of noise; lines up the chairs pretending it is a train; hides under the table; walks on piles of cushions; at the end of the day, he is only two years old.

"Let me take the washing out of the machine and then we'll leave."

The girl, with a large smile on her face, starts to pirouette like a ballerina and then follows her mother to the laundry room. Amina's hands are moving fast, automatically grabbing piles of tiny socks, underwear, t-shirts, trousers to hang on the clotheshorse. The sense of cleanliness is accentuated by the spring fragrance of the fabric softener.

Taha, barefoot, is scattering cornflakes on the floor, singing "*Giro-giro-tondo*".

I look at my watch, "Amina, we'd better leave now if we want to be back by lunchtime."

"Yes *hooyo*, I'm finishing off now."

"Nabila, are you ready? I'll prepare Taha, let's hurry."

Nabila is running up the stairs, to her room, "*Nonna*, I'm going to wear it too." She giggles at me.

"What are you going to wear?"

"The *hijab*, like you."

She takes me by surprise. I know she loves headscarves; when she was a little girl, she used to open my drawers and play with them. She dragged long colourful silky scarves across the room , put them on her head and wrapped her dolls in them. Now she wears it to pray with her mum in the intimacy of their home in the evenings. She collects them. During our last trip to the UK, she went crazy choosing from all the variety she found in the Islamic shop.

But she has never worn a headscarf outside the house, except when we went for the first time to the Central Mosque in London. At the sight of the golden dome, she told me, "*Nonna* it is so beautiful!"

The only prayer place she knew was a cold rectangular space squeezed within four walls, with a floral carpet and neon lights hanging from the ceiling. No sign of the beauty of Islamic architecture and calligraphy. No sign of a fountain and a garden surrounding the building, only dull flat warehouses in a suburb of the city.

In the United Kingdom she met many different people. The whole world gathered on this unique island. Travelling on double-decker buses, my granddaughter was absorbing a whole new experience.

She is back, covered in sky blue with little silver stars on her forehead and a fringe of thick brown shiny natural hair is sticking out. She looks at me, "Do I have to cover all of my hair?"

She is trying to push back her fringe.

"My darling, it is not important, you have not reached the age of a proper *hijab*; you can keep it as you wish".

"Then I want to cover my hair," she decides.

I button Taha's jacket, my daughter holds the car keys and closes the door behind her. I put the child safely in his proper seat while Amina folds the buggy and puts it in the back of the vehicle. Finally we make a move. There is traffic, there is always traffic, and the Saturday market makes it worse. They close the main road to create a space for the stalls. We pass people carrying shopping bags, full of fruit and vegetables, shoes, handbags, flowers, aromatic plants; women jiggling buggies through the crowd; the smell of fried fish and roasted chicken mingle like old friends who meet at a party.

We are heading to a store in the next village, a few miles away. We do not want to waste time in one of those big shopping centres that are bullying the countryside.

In this small shop you can find almost every thing from toys to stationery, clothing, make-up for teens, and oddities that enchant youngsters. Nabila knows every corner of this shop and she has already seen the pink *monopattino*, exactly the one she desires.

We park the car near the cemetery under a row of cypress trees. Summer is ending, the air is cool. Lazy clouds are pushing for some rain.

Amina is putting her son in the buggy. Nabila can't wait. She is hopping, she speeds her steps and her veil moves, letting her hair frame her happy face. She is stunning.

Amina meets an old friend and they stop to chat, we enter the shop.

We pass by a couple and I hear the lady saying in a harsh voice, "Now they force little girls to wear that thing on their head!"

I cannot believe my ears. I am hurt. I turn towards the woman, I am convinced that when people meet and have the chance to talk they can build bridges and wipe out misconceptions.

Keeping calm and putting on my best smile I tell her, "*Signora*, nobody forced my granddaughter to wear the scarf. Children like to experiment, to imitate, it is a game; they want to have fun."

The sturdy woman is wearing an old-fashioned jacket that has become tight; she looks at me, astonished. She did not expect me to speak Italian. After a few seconds, she barks at me, "I do not approve of your customs. I was born here, my father was born here, my grandfather was born here. This is my country and you people have to adjust!"

These words are like a slap on my face. Her eyes are full of hate; she is like a wall, she does not want to hear; my words will only bounce back.

Nabila is standing next to me, holding my hand, her face full of questions. Her happiness entrenched. I squeeze her hand softly and brush her with my affection.

How dare this woman rob the joy from my child? How can I protect my little girl?

I did not want to hear any more rubbish; before I turned my back to her, I said, "*Signora* I wear a headscarf as, for me, it is a religious duty; I can't change my belief for you. I wanted to have a civilised discussion, but it seems to me that it's impossible to reason with a person with your ideas."

We go towards the owner of the store, she heard everything. Trying to make me feel better, she says, "*Signora* don't bother, some people think like this. And then you, *signora*, aren't covered like those who have only their eyes on show. For those women, it's right that the law bans them from walking in the streets".

I shake my head; I thought she could understand, but realise she has her prejudice too.

I keep my voice as natural as possible, "*Signora*, I was in London this summer and saw women in *niqab* driving; it is normal there, you just have to get used to it."

From the way she stares at me I do not think I convinced her. Nabila gets her pink scooter and Taha finds a train. We leave the shop. My daughter knows there is something bothering me, but I do not want to speak in front of the children. Nabila wants to try her scooter as soon we reach home; Taha is fiddling with the seat belt, trying to free himself. My eyes are glued on the road; I am blind to the scenery: traffic, pedestrians, trees, buildings, drops of rain on the windshield. The voices in the car do not reach me, I am immersed in my own thoughts, still hurt; I feel like a pressure cooker that wants to pour out loads of words. Questions whining in my brain, struggling to have an answer.

How can my grandchildren grow up in a country where they are judged by the way they dress?

Why this stigma on a religious symbol?

Why are other people dictating what Islam is?

What is going on? Why are some politicians in the West becoming so intolerant?

Why this scare mongering about a piece of cloth?

The Virgin Mary, in all the paintings and frescoes of every church around the world, is wearing a *hijab*. Is she dangerous?

If this woman knew that my daughter and my grandchildren were born in Italy, that my parents are buried under the *tricolore* flag and my nursery rhymes are dusted with snow the scent of pine trees and the taste of apple; that my first heroes were Christopher Columbus and Mazzini; that Pinocchio was the book I treasured the most and that, when I sang along with Gianni Morandi, his songs brought tears to my eyes as a teenager.

All of this happened thousands of kilometres away from Italy, in Mogadishu, where the mango juice made my fingers sticky and the sea breeze tickled my porcs, while contented seagulls fluttered high in the blue sky; would she still think of me as a second class citizen?

Far From Mogadishu, 20 Years Later

"I would so much like to feel that sense of lightness that we usually feel after crying! It is a feeling that we all remember, but that I am unable to experience despite my crying. Perhaps it depends on the fact that my crying is tearless.

I cry for my city that no longer exists, for a people that suffers. For a land that is destroyed, for men who have gone mad, for the dead animals. I cry because the only sounds that I hear are the whistles of bullets, the exploding of bombs and the bazooka strikes that alternate with screams, weeping, crying and death litanies.

I cry because I have no future, because the smell of death scares me. I cry because I do not want my hope to die."

In 1994 I ended *Lontano da Mogadiscio* with these words. For twenty-two years I have hoped that the war would come to and end and that everything would flourish again. In my dark moments I asked myself if Mogadishu, the city where I was born, bred, got married and became a mother, really existed, or if it was my memory that was betraying me.

To prove myself I travelled a lot, not only physically but also virtually. By word of mouth, international phone calls, Skype, e-mails and Internet, I constantly tried to locate extended family members, old friends, acquaintances and schoolmates. I could not trust my memory, I had to hear the truth from others; I wanted to find names, faces and words... their words, their memories.

Voices from the diaspora that reached me from Australia, Norway, the United States, South Africa and the corners of the world gave me the proof: the Mogadishu that I always carry with me really existed. It lives and buzzes in the veins, in the love and remembrance of thousands of people who lived there. They are strong voices that can dominate every image of death, violence, destruction and hate.

A great responsibility is incumbent on us who have had the fortune to experience that Mogadishu and were nourished by the love of Somalia, our land, our mother: we have the duty to pass on to the younger generation who were born in the dark years of the war, all the love and the brotherhood that we witnessed.

Since August 1st 2012, the hope for a rebirth is tangible. Somalia is a country recognised again by the international community. The Somali Federal Republic has been born. I feel relief now that the positive spotlight of the media is on this country, which was stigmatised for years by negative images. At the Olympic Games, in London, I waited with trepidation to see the Somali flag paraded. It touched my heart. The small delegation passed unnoticed, but the bright side is that the games concluded with the British athlete of Somali origin, Mohamed Farah, known as Mo, winning a double gold medal for the United Kingdom.

In London, on May 7th 2013, a very important conference was held. The United Kingdom took on a commitment to help the Somali Federal government, and it is the first country to reopen its embassy in Mogadishu.

Although there is still sporadic news of terrorist attacks aimed at destabilizing the country, images coming from the capital are comforting and give great hope to the people of the diaspora. The ones who live in Somalia got back their enthusiasm and the aim to reconstruct. The goal to turn a page is at our fingertips, now like never before. I pray and wish for a future of peace and prosperity for my country.

As a citizen of the world, I travel a lot and observe with a critical eye the changes that have been going on in the last twenty years in my other country, Italy.

I am ashamed of how little has been done regarding hospitality and integration.

The Federal Republic of Somalia offers great opportunities for investment today, since it is rich in natural resources including minerals and oil, fertile lands, fishable seas, and cattle to export. The people of the Somali diaspora can offer significant human resources as they have acquired know-how and contacts in countries that are industrially developed throughout these years of pain and separation within families.

In my view, Italy can have a significant role in this rebirth only if it aims at initiating an honest and fair partnership with Somalia. So far, the relationship between my two countries has been different: Italy has polluted the territory, sold weapons and maintained a controversial policy about refugees.

Can Italy afford to miss a big chance like this? Italy is at a crossroads; now only the old dinosaurs of my generation speak Italian or remember the language of Dante. Do we want that a worn-out Triumphal Arch covered with bullet holes, a choking Fiat 682 engine truck, a nostalgic colonial song and maybe a faded sign in Italian to be all that reminds us of a link that is gone?

The Rise of a New Dawn

A new dawn rises,
let's bury weapons,
hatred,
clan divisions,
ignorance,
injustice,
personal interest.

A new dawn rises,
let's leave behind
the bitter taste
of being a refugee,
of the young who die without a name and a gravestone,
swallowed by the sea and by the desert.

A new dawn rises,
let's build our country
with pride,
dignity,
respect.

A new dawn rises,
let's cure our wounds
with love,
brotherhood,
forgiveness,
faith.

The End

"A Dialogue that Knows no Border between Nationality, Race or Culture": Themes, Impact and the Critical Reception of Far from Mogadishu.[113]

Simone Brioni

IMLR Visiting Fellow

University of London

Translating hits nerves in the text; elements emerge that did not stand out, which maybe in the original language we did not even notice if they were there or not. So the translation is almost a new text, in fact; it has the power, in my eyes, of a new text.[114]

Shirin Ramzanali Fazel's *Far from Mogadishu* was published almost twenty years ago, in 1994, and reprinted once, in 1999.[115] The current republication is an expanded bilingual version (in Italian and English) that revisits that text. Although it was distributed by a small publisher, *Far from Mogadishu* is crucial in the contemporary literary panorama for at least three reasons: the contribution to decolonising Italian memory, the testimony of a black person's experience living in Italy from the seventies to the nineties (and in the present version, to the 2000s), and the memory of a Mogadishu destroyed by a devastating civil war beginning in 1991, in view of a possible reconstruction of Somalia.

Together with *Aulò. Canto Poesia dell'Eritrea* by Ribka Sibhatu (1993)[116] and the autobiographical account *Andiamo a spasso? Scirscir'n demna* by Maria Abebù Viarengo (1992),[117] *Far from Mogadishu* was one of the first texts to present from the point of view of the colonised Italian colonial history, a period about which a guilty amnesia is in force. Somalia was an Italian protectorate from 1885 to 1905. It later became a colony, included in the empire from 1936 until the end of the Second World War. From 1950 to 1960, the United Nations entrusted the former colonisers with the administration of Somalia (AFIS). The AFIS was a sort of colonialism with a time limit, where Italy left administrators already present in the territory, mostly fascists, in the ex-colony.[118] Shirin[119] was born in this period, to be precise in 1953; she had a Somali mother and a Pakistani father, and studied "in middle schools and high schools [...] which were [...] run directly from Rome by the Minister of State Education [...] in the same way as any state school operating in Italian territory".[120] *In Far from Mogadishu*, Shirin says that "[she] studied Italian language at school" in Somalia,[121] as well as "Garibaldi, Mazzini and their struggle for Italian unification", and she "appreciated [...] Pietro Germi [...] the songs of Modugno, Mina, Gianni Morandi [and] Dante, Pavese, and Pirandello's writings".[122]

Italy and Somalia's histories do not simply intertwine during the period of the AFIS. For example, the dictatorship of Siad Barre (1969-1991) was supported by Italy,[123] and Somalia was also the primary destination for Italian resources in the post-war cooperation.[124] The publication of *Far from Mogadishu* corresponds to another important episode in the relationship between Italy and Somalia, that is to say the murder of the television news journalist Ilaria Alpi and the cameraman Miran Hrovatin in Mogadishu. As recent inquiries seem to demonstrate, they were both investigating the traffic of arms coming from Italy and sold in Somalia in exchange for the removal of illicit waste.[125] That investigation tried to clarify the role of Italian producers in the arms used in the Somali civil war, which started in 1991 with the deposition of Siad Barre and continued until a few months ago, when the process of the reconstruction of the new Somali state began. *Far from Mogadishu* bears witness to the relationship between Italy and Somalia, also showing that "this proximity is rarely reciprocal [as] Somalia is largely an unknown reality in contemporary Italy".[126]

Far from Mogadishu started a process of revision of the colonial past that was then also dealt with independently by other Italian writers including, to mention just a few of the more well-known names, Cristina Ali Farah, Enrico Brizzi, Andrea Camilleri, Franca Cavagnoli, Erminia dell'Oro, Gabriella Ghermandi, Carlo Lucarelli, Igiaba Scego, and two of the members of the Wu Ming collective, whose works were produced "with four hands".[127] Some of these authors acknowledged the influence of Shirin's work in their novels and in the Italian literary *Zeitgeist* in the years after. For example, Igiaba Scego defined Shirin as "an example that inspired the new generation of migrant writers",[128] and stated that "her words contain all the determination of Somali women. Strong and independent women, who have shouldered the fate of a country at war".[129] Some sections of Wu Ming 2 and Antar Mohamed's *Timira. Romanzo Meticcio* were also inspired by the work of Shirin,[130] in particular her second novel *Clouds on the Equator* (2010),[131] a text which focuses on the story of a *meticcio* girl abandoned by her father during the AFIS period, who grows up in a Catholic orphanage and is rejected by both the communities she belongs to.

Far from Mogadishu played a fundamental role in decolonising the Italian imaginary, and in finally coming to terms with a history which research begun in the seventies showed to be full of atrocious crimes. Indeed, the Italians in Africa created concentration and forced labour camps,[132] and massively and indiscriminately used chemical weapons against civilians.[133] The meaning and importance of the present publication seems to be once more confirmed by the recent attempt to name a mausoleum at Affile, in the province of Rome, after the facist war criminal Rodolfo Graziani, which demonstrates how historical evidence did not manage to find its way into the Italians' collective consciousness.

Secondly, Shirin's text is the testimony of a black person's life story in Northern Italy, first in Novara (from 1971 to 1976) and then near Vicenza (where the writer has lived since 1985), in a period which precedes more widespread African immigration to these areas. *Far from Mogadishu* is one of the first novels written in the Italian language to narrate an experience of migration without the help of an Italian co-author in order to guarantee the volume's linguistic correctness, in contrast to the first novels about immigration published at the beginning of the nineties.[134] Moreover, Shirin's is a female voice, which aims to bring to light the role of women in history since, as the writer pointed out in an interview, they "keep together the various threads of family and friends, take care of the old people, and the children. It is always the women who keep the traditions, the memories, the taste of food, who know how to tell their stories and are not afraid of crying then smiling again. Women are the link between the past, present and future".[135]

The theme of migration is central to Shirin's work and her gaze allows us to re-read Italy's recent history from the perspective of someone who experienced the problems of many immigrants, revealing a substantial continuity in the distinterest for their political and social recognition in the last twenty years.[136] However, assuming that Shirin's experience of migration might be a paradigm to understand that of other immigrants is misleading for at least two reasons. Firstly, when Shirin arrived in Italy in 1971 she had moved to a country where she was already a "citizen" thanks to her marriage in 1970 (note that at that time Italian citizenship was given through marriage only to the spouse of an Italian male).[137] Secondly, Shirin left Somalia for "political reasons"[138] rather than economic ones like a large number of African immigrants in Italy: hers was an exile, a one-way trip, decided because of the military dictatorship and the civil war. After the coup in 1969, Siad Barre had actually ordered out of the country those who did not own a Somali passport, which the writer did not have due to her Pakistani father.

Although Shirin's experience is different from that of many other immigrants, *Far from Mogadishu* can be read as the barometer of the drift towards increasing racism against immigrants in Italy in the last few years. Whilst the country Shirin arrived in was ignorant and curious about immigrants, the one where she found herself living in the nineties after having opened a restaurant in Kenya (from 1996 to 2004) and which she left in 2010 to go to the United Kingdom, is described as clearly xenophobic.[139] Despite this, Shirin never *really* distanced herself from Italy, since it was there she formed most of her attachments and bought her own house. The choice to republish this text is testimony to this connection, as well as to the writer's commitment to influence change in the current social situation in Italy.

A third reason for the interest in this editorial project is linked to the fact that *Far from Mogadishu* narrates the recent history of Somalia and the experience of diaspora from a literary perspective. *Far from*

Mogadishu is a valid example of the dynamic character of diasporic writing, of its forced adaptability to historical and geographical changes, and its becoming "the means through which [...] writers can find a space and discuss their own self and the ways that their multilayered cultural identity is formed".[140] Texts by writers from the Somali diaspora represent the heritage of a culture which has also proliferated in written form in other languages, given that Somali has been written as a codified alphabet since 1972.[141] For this reason it should be noted that, having emigrated to Italy before this date, Shirin can write better in Italian than in Somali, despite being able to speak it perfectly.

In particular, this novel narrates the pain connected to the destruction of Mogadishu, Shirin's native city, which the writer describes with these words: "When the civil war broke out in 1991 I was in Italy, it felt like I was going mad, seeing my city bombarded, reduced to a pile of rubble, it was as if they had taken away my identity. Places dear to me that had formed who I was had become dust, erased forever [...] Unfortunately today it is still [...] a wound that has never healed. And this is not only for me but for all the Somali diaspora".[142] Mogadishu is a city that exists in the stories of its inhabitants, now displaced in various parts of the world, and only thanks to their memories can it be reconstructed. *Far from Mogadishu* can be credited with drawing attention to the civil war in Somalia without the sensationalist rhetoric of the western media, and above all with speaking about the thousand-year coexistence of different cultures which was there before it.[143]

Even the most renowned Somali author in the Anglophone world, Nuruddin Farah, acknowledged that Shirin was "the first [author] to write a book about the civil war from a Somali perspective",[144] through the words of the protagonist of his novel Links (2004), Jeebleh. Reading *Far from Mogadishu,* Jeebleh "was pleased that Somalis were recording their ideas about themselves and their country, sometimes in their own language, sometimes in foreign tongues. These efforts, meagre as they might seem, pointed to the gaps in the world's knowledge about Somalia. Reading the slim volume had been salutary, because unlike many books by authors with clan-sharpened axes to grind, this was not a grievance-driven pamphlet".[145] As Lorenzo Mari has pointed out, Nuruddin Farah suggests that *Far from Mogadishu* allows us to understand the links between the members of the Somali diaspora and "the transnational debate about Somalia and Somali postcolonial literature",[146] showing "the existing gaps not only in Italian postcolonial knowledge, but also in the world's knowledge regarding Somalia at the time of the *Restore Hope* operation, which is encapsulated by the event of *Black Hawk Down*, in October 1993".[147]

Two characters in Links, Jeebleh and Shanta, also discuss how Shirin was able to link her Somali origins to Persian ones, noting that her name and part of her family originated from there.[148] According to Mari, these characters praise Shirin for "[seeing herself] as part of 'one big Somali family'", "while many Somalis, re-tribalised by the colonial administration, by Barre's politics and by the clan-based violence of the civil war, aren't able to".[149] This passage of *Links* is useful for understanding how the definition of the author's identity in *Far from Mogadishu* can change in relation to the context in which the novel is read. Whilst Shirin has often been defined as a "Somali" and "migrant" writer in Italy, the two characters in *Links* talk about her as a second generation Somali writer – her father was born in Zanzibar in 1917, and moved to Somalia in 1945 –, and for this reason it is extrinsic to the clanism that erupts in the country during the civil war.

For (at least) these three reasons, writing the foreword to *Far from Mogadishu* is a difficult responsibility, but one which can take advantage of a lively critical debate. At the same time, the reprinting of a text that catalysed the attention of many literary scholars in the last twenty years can provide the opportunity to reflect on the development of migrant writing in Italian. In particular, the retrospective reading of the introduction to the first edition of *Far from Mogadishu* by Alessandra Atti di Sarro provides useful information about a critical discourse dominant at the beginning of the nineties and later widely called into question, which I believe managed to lead some readers astray regarding the intentions and the potentialities of this text.

To clarify, my analysis does not wish to negate the commendable and pioneering work of this journalist, who can also be credited with finding a publisher for the text. Re-reading this introduction "in hindsight", should above all be a reminder not to trust paratexts too much (including the current one), and to interrogate the text independently. It should also be noted that whilst this afterword aims to collect and examine the varied critical responses to *Far from Mogadishu* (often quite difficult to track down and written both in English and Italian), Atti di Sarro's introduction had a completely different function, that is to support and present to an audience of compatriots the novelty of a text written in Italian by an author of non-Italian origin.

Atti di Sarro's introduction has a good grasp of Shirin's ability to develop "a dialogue that knows no border between nationality, race or culture".[150] However, at the same time the journalist presents the author as an immigrant, whose story can be assimilated into a wider dynamic of economic migration: "we find ourselves, us from the Old Continent, crowded with another type of visitor. They are no longer – from the North – ineffable rich tourists greedy for culture and artistic beauty, rather – from the South – droves of poor things looking for a bit of prosperity".[151] Atti di Sarro also underlines the "vulnerability" of these immigrants, who "can only count on the hospitality that others can offer them".[152] This condition does not seem to represent that of Shirin, who arrived in "a country [she] knew",[153] curious to confirm that the idea she had got of Italy from books was true.[154] Shirin is a cosmopolitan intellectual – with a cosmopolitanism which she associates several times with her religion, Islam –,[155] who since 1976 has travelled to Zambia, the United States (where the writer lived for two years, from 1987 to 1989), Saudi Arabia, Canada, Kenya, and Zanzibar. For Shirin the travel dimension is not therefore exclusively connected to migration, but also to tourism. A significant section of *Far from Mogadishu* entitled "The suitcase"[156] "measures the capacity of migrant memory by comparing the tourist's and the immigrant's suitcase",[157] which contain the souvenirs bought in an exotic destination and all the memories of a land perhaps left forever respectively.[158] Thus Luigi Marfé defined *Far from Mogadishu* as a "counter-travel book"; it "[stages] a sort of Grand Tour in reverse, which, instead of describing Italy as the land of classical culture, shows the contradictions of its grassroots, especially with regard to the theme of how foreigners are received".[159] In other words, *Far from Mogadishu* overturns some of the topoi of tourist discourse, such as "the dialectics between the observer – who is not European, but African – and the observed – who are not African, but Italian natives".[160]

Furthermore, the introduction tends to create a dichotomous opposition between the immigrants' culture and "Western culture", referring to the readers as a cohesive group of which Atti di Sarro is part: "Us westerners".[161] This opposition is accentuated by the cover of the 1994 edition which shows the face of a young African woman with very dark skin, her head covered by a veil clearly of oriental craftsmanship, contributing to the identification of the author of *Far from Mogadishu* as foreign. In open opposition to this paratext, the cover of the present edition instead bears witness to the autobiographical character of *Far from Mogadishu*.

The description of the borders of Italy and Somalia found in *Far from Mogadishu* seems to have cultural and geographical borders that are certainly less clear-cut than the first edition's paratextual apparatus indicates. According to Roberta di Carmine, "the 'walls' [Shirin] is referring to at the beginning of her text, symbolically resemble those borders – national, political, social, and cultural – which have slowly and inevitably prevented individuals [from revealing but also from defining] their own identity".[162] Moreover, when Shirin sees the images of the destruction of Mogadishu on television she feels part of the tragedy happening to her people,[163] but at the same time represents herself as "a white observer separated from this tragedy",[164] since she is "part of a privileged group whose cultural whiteness has contaminated the interpretation of her own past".[165] Graziella Parati, who has commented in detail on this significant passage of the text, has underlined that Shirin describes multiple belongings, delineating her identity as hybrid: "starting from a description of her familial community at the dinner table, identified as an initial 'us', [Shirin] changes the representation of community, of the 'us', beyond the domestic sphere into a public 'us' that is not defined along colour lines. That 'us' made of people watching the same images on Italian television involves an elaboration of the concept of sameness that includes those who participate in and validate narratives on otherness that seem so distant on television. [...] Same and different become [...] permeable entities that collaborate in defining the large community she is addressing. [Shirin] expresses the need for a redefinition of community and for a collective act of witnessing the construction of multicultural Italian identities".[166]

The way in which Shirin positions herself distant from or close to Italy or Somalia is also entirely unique. Contrary to the title, the capital of Somalia is never truly far, but rather "is narrated in the present tense, yet [Shirin]'s own life in Somalia, as detailed in Parte prima, is recounted in the past tense with the almost complete non-appearance of its author".[167] The ambiguous relationship that Shirin, an "Italian with dark skin",[168] has with her country of which she is a resident and citizen is well expressed in this passage of *Far from Mogadishu*: "I am an Italian citizen, I participate in and experience the problems, the suffering that all Italians face every day. I contribute to the life and the evolution of this country. Now that both my parents are buried here, I feel even more tied to this land. Italy is my home; my relationships are here, my friends. Even so, there is always someone who reminds me that I am an intruder, an anomaly".[169]

What is delineated in *Far from Mogadishu* is therefore a dynamic of double belonging together with double unbelonging. Lucia Benchouiha describes it more precisely with these words: "the structural and geographical divisions [...] suggest a doubling but also a fragmented notion of national identification [...] from somewhere 'in-between' the two countries, both 'here' and 'there', yet incongruously neither entirely 'there' nor wholly 'here'. The fracturing of the setting and organisation of the text has similar repercussions for perceptions of time in this narrative since the partitions between the 'there' (Somalia) and the 'here' (Italy) are similarly expressed in a temporal fashion between the 'before/then' (Somalia) and the 'after/now' (Italy)".[170] In an article that focuses on similar issues, Nathan Vetri analyses a passage of the text in which it talks about the birth of a *meticcio* boy called Michele,[171] and argues that Shirin indicates a third way of living in a new country, beyond the dichotomous opposition between integration and rejection, that is "suspension, achieved primarily through the ambiguity of the characters that inhabit the Italian spaces within texts. [...] their bodies are successfully capable of negotiating outside the realms of Italianess and non, thus dissolving essentialist dichotomies of 'us' and 'them', of 'same' and 'other'".[172]

Similarly, *Far from Mogadishu* describes the concept of home as "a plury- or trans-local concept".[173] According to Jennifer Burns, the references to the life of Shirin in different towns "underscore this notion that home is a practice of negotiating and (re)constructing affective attachments in and between places. Since all those locations are collectively defined by being 'lontano da Mogadiscio', however, the text also cements the notion that there is an origin, an Ur-home, to which all others refer in a shifting economy of affects".[174] In other words, the concept of home represented in the novel can be "less accurately grasped according to a vertical model, where the place of origin is buried deep in a past which is also geographically distant, than by a notion of horizontality, whereby different homes are layered and superimposed over one another as sites of historical memory and experience, both for the individual and the nation or culture, at the same time as they offer sites of belonging for the present and future".[175] *Lontano da Mogadiscio* not only recreates the memory of Mogadishu, but also brings the town to life in the here and now, engaging the reader emotively in its reconstruction: "Home – Mogadishu – is all-pervasive in the text, but it is a home which is both lost in the past and dynamically visible in the present, and at the same time, a home which is radically, sometimes exotically, different and distant from Italy and insistently connected to everyday life in Italy. [...] Home travels with [Shirin] not only as a personal and emotional totem, but rather as an entire, mobile *habitus*; the cultural, political, moral, geographical, and affective reality of her home country".[176]

The introduction to the first edition includes *Far from Mogadishu* in a group of texts written by immigrants in Italian, which it describes as a single corpus, and altogether devoid of discursive complexity: "books like that of Shirin Ramzanali Fazel (and of other immigrant authors before her), [are] bare and simple 'travel' narratives, [...] without charm, in which there are very few are comments, [...] or clear and direct judgements".[177] In other words, Shirin simply talked "about herself to herself, to others, to the world",[178] and it is "nothing more and nothing less than her own story".[179] This judgement seems to be further confirmed by some critical analysis of writings by immigrants in Italian that claimed there was an evolution from a series of autobiographical works, which are more interesting from a sociological rather than literary point of view, to novels with more refined and complex narrative structures.

These models seem to be based on two assumptions that are deep-rooted in Western culture and, as such, they seem inappropriate to be applied to experiences that are not entirely located in one singular cultural context: the distinction between "high" and "low" cultural forms, and that between different literary genres, which are seen as fixed, monolithical and non permeable categories.[180] However, Shirin's successive literary works – which include the novel *Clouds on the Equator* and the short stories *Omdurmann's Secret* (published for the first time in 1995 in the journal "Italian Studies in Southern Africa", and available online since 2009),[181] *Gabriel* (2008),[182] *The Beach* (2008),[183] *Global Village* (2010),[184] *Mukulaal (Cat)* (2010),[185] and *DNA* (2011)[186] –, suggest that *Far from Mogadishu* is not the episodic experience of an immigrant who has become a writer merely because of her life experience. Shirin has used the autobiographical genre among others to talk about "the issues arising in Italian multicultural society", in the same way in which "other Italian authors write about the Mafia and the Camorra".[187]

Moreover, the composite structure into which *Far from Mogadishu* is sub-divided seems to indicate that this work is an autobiography *sui generis*. As Shirin has stated in an interview, *Far from Mogadishu* does not follow a chronological order, but rather links different situations together in relation to the emotions inspired by the narration of the events.[188] The original nucleus of this text was divided into "six parts, each about a subject or a period: the Somalia of her childhood, her arrival in Italy, travels to other countries,

Somalia at war, Somalia and Africa through Italians' eyes, identity and political and ethical commitment".[189] In the new version there are also two unedited sections which deal with Shirin's recent move to the UK. The time periods which intertwine in *Far from Mogadishu* are therefore at least four: the memory of Somalia before 1970 described in 1994, the narration in the present of 1994, the re-reading and re-writing of those parts from the viewpoint of 2013, and the writing in the present of Shirin's daily life in 2013. By doing this, Shirin further complicates the operation of "translating immigration into emigration", through which "displacement" becomes a "re-discovery of the 'place' from which she has been removed".[190]

Although it is based on the life experiences of the author, *Far from Mogadishu* tells a story which transcends the personal.[191] As has been noted before, the 1994 version of *Far from Mogadishu* already described multiple belongings, including for example that of of the television audience who watched Somalia's drama in the west, and of a group discriminated against in Italy because of the colour of their skin. Moreover, Shirin mentioned other members of the Somali diaspora like "Mumina, Dahir, Abdi",[192] who shared their stories and contribute "to undermine the notion of Somalia as the object of other national or regional narratives and to present it rather as the subject of its own narrative, still in the making".[193] The present version also describes a new imaginary community to which Shirin feels she belongs: the one established by other emigrants in Italy and then in the UK, like the woman of Moroccan origin called Leila who the writer meets in Birmingham and who she converses with in Italian.[194]

Because it is simultaneously "a rhapsody of ideas, reflections, biographical notes, political considerations",[195] it is difficult to see *Far from Mogadishu* as being part of a strictly autobiographical genre. For this reason, Loredana Polezzi points out that the hybrid form of the text is linked to the author's complex description of identity: "*Lontano da Mogadiscio* is a patchwork of passages, often less than a page long, which take a multitude of forms: from the poem to the mini-historical essay to the etymological gloss, the anecdote, the list, or the intimate diary entry. [...] the fragmented structure of the [text] is also symptomatic of the fractured personal and collective histories with which [the author identifies]".[196] The literary hybridity of *Far from Mogadishu* has also been underlined by Riannon Noel Welch, who states that this text has "a narrative voice that is at once autobiographical and anthropological (the narrator shuttles between the positions of subject, observer and ethnographic informant), and [she] def[ies] generic classification as travel narrative, journalistic reportage, autobiography or ethnography".[197] Because of these reasons, Jennifer Burns argues that *Far from Mogadishu* is a literary product which is "at once familiar (autobiography, testimony, narrative) and perplexing (all and none of these)".[198] Thanks to its "hybrid potential" and to the narration "not just of stories but also histories, diaries, or testimony", this text represents a clear example of politically committed writing in postmodern Italy.[199]

The unique character of this text is also signalled by the presence of diverse literary genres in the text. For example, *Far from Mogadishu* opens and closes with two poems, "Rainbow" and "The Dawning of a New Day", which was not present in the 1994 version. The centrality of "Rainbow"[200] in the text was clearly recognised by Shirin in an interview with Rebecca Hopkins: "The rainbow for me is both harmony and beauty, different colours which go well together. We are people coming from different countries who must learn to live in harmony. The key word for me is respect for yourself… and for others".[201] This poem is a trace of the very first draft of the text that the writer had conceived before meeting the publisher Datanews to be a diary and a collection of poems entitled *Incense, Myrrh and Gunpowder*.

The first part of the work also distances itself from the autobiographical dimension, and presents more didactic sections aimed at bringing the Italian audience closer to another culture. The knowledge of the other seems crucial to combat intolerance, given that for Shirin racism is the product of "ignorance".[202] Indeed, as the writer states in the poem that opens the book: "if you hated us even before meeting or if you pitied us to relieve your conscience, you have been completely mistaken".[203] The first section of *Far from Mogadishu* describes Somalia as an idyllic world, "a country in which every child would want to grow and play" or a "country of fairytales",[204] repeatedly using the forms "there was" and "there were".[205] This strategic device might have been adopted in order to bridge the gap with a reader used to magnificent descriptions of Africa, like those found for example in Karen Blixen's famous book *Out of Africa*.[206] According to Graziella Parati, this fairy-tale dimension "attempts to neutralize the present destruction of Somalia and the vision of an apocalyptic future",[207] changes in the rest of the novel, where Shirin historicises the unequal power relations that her country of origin has experienced and delivers "a social commentary on how western ideology is responsible for keeping Africa trapped into stereotypical misrepresentations".[208] As Daniele Comberiati points out in relation to Shirin's short story *Mukulaal (Cat)*[209] – but I believe this statement could particularly be applied to the fourth section of *Far from Mogadishu* –, she narrates violence "through a bitter realism"[210] which aims to provoke reflection on the current political situation in Somalia.

Far from Mogadishu therefore seems to be a text which manifests not only an "equal dialogue between cultures of the world",[211] but also a reaction to intolerance, a response to western hegemony, and a linguistic and cultural fracture. In particular, this aspect of *Far from Mogadishu* is made clear by language which is stretched to its limits thanks to the possibilities offered by translation and self-translation. At first glance, *Far from Mogadishu* is written in standard Italian, which is "harmonious, filtered through a veil of sensitivity and lightness, with the main objective of making the reader reflect",[212] and with a style which has been defined as "sober",[213] "light",[214] "poetic and imaginative".[215] For example, Monica Venturini points out that Shirin uses "direct language, a paratactic style which aims at an effective synthesis and at the evocation of the smallest details in a nonlinear flow of memories".[216] The choice of this language appears to be intended to confirm Shirin's linguistic ability in Italian, called into question by many of her compatriots: "[in reply to a question in Italian] the person would look at me and start to articulate words clearly, using verbs in infinite in a loud voice".[217]

However, the linguistic particularity of *Far from Mogadishu* is found in the way in which Italian and Somali dialogue in the text. The presence of Somali words in the Italian text does not only show "the author's determination to maintain a direct and vivid connection with [her] cultural and linguistic roots",[218] but also and above all the desire to re-shape Italian, making it welcoming to other languages, and keeping the Somali language alive in other cultural contexts. In other words, *Far from Mogadishu* signals a lack of attachment exclusively to a nostalgic dimension of Somalia in linguistic terms too.

The complex linguistic intersection in this text can be better understood in relation to some of the choices made by the publishers, which differentiate the present edition from the first edition, such as the translation of Somali words inserted into the text rather than into footnotes, and the double form of Italian-English. The 1994 edition of *Far from Mogadishu* was aimed at an audience unused to coming across foreign words in an Italian text. Including the translation of Somali expressions in footnotes meant that the readers had to deal with a language they did not know, and it also complicated the expressive form of the text. Yet Lucie Benchouiha has argued that this communicative device had the effect of making the Somali expressions "more unfamiliar and alien to her readers since the very foreignness of some of [Shirin]'s language is actually multiplied through this act of italicising, footnoting, and translating these terms. This method of dealing with language therefore draws attention to the linguistic hybridity of the narrative and, as a result, highlights a different, non-Italian identity for the author of this work".[219] This comment allows us to understand how the author's construction of identity takes place also through language and the way in which this is presented to the reader. The footnotes in the first version also had the effect of interrupting the flow of reading, presenting Somali as an intrusive presence within the Italian text and the author of the text as an intruder within the Italian social context.

By positioning the Somali expressions directly in the text and making them dialogue with the Italian, this edition of *Far from Mogadishu* differentiates itself from that of 1994, which instead seems to give Italian a greater importance in meaning compared to Somali by using footnotes. The choice of a different translation strategy in the present edition of the text seems to better reflect both the description of identity which the author herself offers – that is of a person for whom "Somali and Italian culture have always been mixed together [and] the two idioms do not [have] border lines" –,[220] and the changed conditions in Italy, in which immigration is no longer a new phenomenon, and the public is increasingly used to linguistic deterritorialisation.

The original work on Shirin's language found a natural development when the writer came to live in Birmingham, in the UK, and translated her novel into English, first publishing part of it in a magazine.[221] The operation of translation then led to the re-writing of the Italian work, to the addition of some parts not present in the original version ("The Triumphal Arch", *Stasera mi butto*, "The Well", "The Purse"), and to the modification of the first three chapters of the book. The new parts in Italian were again translated (or in some cases re-written) into English. This recent work on the text makes another aspect already present in the 1994 edition even more explicit, that is the close relationship that the writing of *Far from Mogadishu* has with linguistic and cultural translation.

If it is read in the light of a recent article by Loredana Polezzi,[222] Shirin's work can also be placed alongside that of other Italian authors who have reflected on the fragmentary, polyphonic and polycentric character of language, and have placed intercultural translation and reflection on mobility at the centre of their work. For a partial intersection of their trajectories of migration, take for example Luigi Meneghello, who moved from a village in the Veneto region of Italy not far from Shirin's house to the UK. Although they come from completely different cultural backgrounds, this writer and Shirin share the same reflection on the heterogeneity that characterises each national context, beyond attempts to make literary history conform to a homogenous and monoglossic template.

In its new garb *Far from Mogadishu* aims to narrate a life experience which crosses physical, political and cultural boundaries to a transnational audience. *Far from Mogadishu* is a text which brings hope to Somalis, wherever they are, and in which the memory of "that" Mogadishu survives. A text which "can contribute to the literary cultures of Italy (and of Europe) in a powerful and political way that problematises our critical and intellectual convictions (or presumptions)".[223] A text which escapes easy categorisation, and which at a distance of twenty years keeps intact its surprising vitality and its ability to narrate the world in which we live from a perspective that is innovative, lucid and touching.

Translated by Kate Willman.

References:

113 I would like to thank the Italian Deparment, the Humanities Research Centre and the Institute of Advanced Studies at the Universiy of Warwick for supporting three research projects which invited Shirin Ramzanali Fazel as a guest: 'Kaleidoscope: New Perspectives on the Humanities' (28-29 May 2011), 'The Italian Trusteeship in Somalia (AFIS) and Beyond' (18 January 2012), and 'Migration, Discrimination and Belonging: Transnational Spaces in Postcolonial Europe' (6 March 2013).

114 Luigi Meneghello, *Materia di Reading e altri reperti*, Milano, Rizzoli, 2005, p. 249 [my translation].

115 Shirin Ramzanali Fazel, *Lontano da Mogadiscio*, Roma, Datanews, 1994.

116 Ribka Sibhatu, *Aulò. Canto poesia dell'Eritrea*, Roma, Sinnos, 1993.

117 Maria Abebù Viarengo, *Andiamo a spasso? Scirscir'n demna*, in "Linea d'ombra" 54 (1992), pp. 75-128.

118 See Antonio Maria Morone, *L'ultima colonia: Come l'Italia è ritornata in Somalia 1950- 1960*, Roma-Bari, Laterza, 2011.

119 I refer to names of Arab, Somali and Tigrinya and Kikuyu origin using their first name according to the correct form used in those languages. The same criterium was applied in the bibliography. I chose this criterium, borrowed from African studies, to avoid the ambiguity with which scholars have referred to this writer so far using different forms, such as "Ramzanali, Fazel Shirin" or "Ramzanali Fazel, Shirin".

120 Rebecca Hopkins, *Somalia: passato, presente e futuro. Intervista con la scrittrice Shirin Ramzanali Fazel*, in "El-ghibli. Rivista online di letteratura della migrazione" 18 (2007), http://www.el-ghibli.provincia.bologna.it/id_1-issue_04_18-section_6-index_pos_1.html [accessed 2 August 2013; my translation].

121 Shirin Ramzanali Fazel, *Lontano da Mogadiscio. Far From Mogadishu*, Simone Brioni (ed.), Milano, Laurana, 2013, p. 220.

122 Ibid.

123 See Angelo Del Boca, *Una sconfitta dell'intelligenza. Italia e Somalia*, Roma-Bari, Laterza, 1993.

124 See Paolo Tripodi, *The Colonial Legacy in Somalia: Rome and Mogadishu: from Colonial Administration to Operation Restore Hope*, London, Palgrave-Mcmillan, 1999, pp.106-137.

125 See Roberto Scardova (ed.), *Carte false: l'assassinio di Ilaria Alpi e Miran Hrovatin. Quindici anni senza verità*, Roma, Ambiente, 2009.

126 Lidia Curti, *Voices of a Minor Empire: Migrant Women Writers in Contemporary Italy*, in *The Cultures of Italian Migration*, Graziella Parati, Anthony Julian Tamburri (eds.), Madison, Fairleigh Dickinson University Press, 2011, pp.45-58.

127 For a list of some of the films and texts that have dealt with this theme in the last twenty years see Simone Brioni, *Coincidenze, in Somalitalia. Quattro vie per Mogadiscio/Somalitalia. Four Roads to Mogadishu*, Simone Brioni (ed.), Roma, Kimerafilm, 2012 [this section is included in the documentary *Per un discorso postcoloniale italiano: parole chiave]*. Wu Ming 1 and Roberto Santachiara's *Point Lenana* has not been included in this list as it was published in 2013. See See Wu Ming 1 and Roberto Santachiara, *Point Lenana*, Torino, Einaudi, 2013.

128 Igiaba Scego, *Shirin Ramzanali F. Scrittrice Nomade*, in "Internazionale" 732 (22 Febbraio 2008), p. 60 [my translation].

129 Ibid., p. 62 [my translation].

130 Wu Ming 2 and Antar Mohamed, Timira. Romanzo Meticcio, Torino, Einaudi, 2012, p. 516.

131 Shirin Ramzanali Fazel, *Nuvole sull'equatore. Gli italiani dimenticati. Una storia*, Cuneo, Nerosubianco, 2010.

132 A map of these camps is available on the website *I campi fascisti: Dalle guerre in Africa alla Repubblica di Salò*, www.campifascisti.it [accessed 2 August 2013].

133 See Angelo del Boca, *I crimini del colonialismo fascista*, in *Le guerre coloniali del fascismo*, Angelo Del Boca (ed.), Roma-Bari, Laterza, 1991, pp. 232-255.

134 For an analysis of collaborative texts written in this period see the following articles: Jennifer Burns, *Frontiere nel testo: autori, collaborazioni e mediazioni nella scrittura italofona della migrazione,* in Jennifer Burns, Loredana Polezzi (eds.), *Borderlines: Migrazioni e identità nel Novecento*, Isernia, Cosmo Iannone, 2003, pp. 203-212; Jennifer Burns, Outside *Voices Within: Immigration Literature in Italian*, in Trends in Contemporary Italian Narrative 1980-2007, in Ania Gillian, Ann Hallamore Caesar (eds.), Cambridge, Cambridge Scholars, 2007, pp. 136-154; Sharon Wood, *A «Quattro Mani»: Collaboration in Italian Immigrant Literature*, in Sara Bigliazzi, Sharon Wood (eds.), *Collaboration in the Arts from the Middle Ages to the Present*, Ashgate, Aldershot, 2006, pp. 151-162.

135 Monica Venturini *CONTROCÀNONe. Per una cartografia della scrittura coloniale e postcoloniale italiana*, Roma, Aracne, 2010, p. 142 [my translation].

136 See Wu Ming, *Primavera Migrante*, in "*Internazionale*" (4 April 2013), http://www.internazionale.it/opinioni/wu-ming/2013/04/04/primavera-migrante/ [accessed 2 August 2013].

137 Shirin Ramzanali Fazel, *Lontano da Mogadiscio. Far From Mogadishu*, cit., p. 300.

138 Rebecca Hopkins, cit. [my translation].

139 See Shirin Ramzanali Fazel, *Le storie intrecciate della diaspora somala/The Intervowen Stories of Somali Diaspora*, in *Somalitalia: Quattro Vie per Mogadiscio. Somalitalia: Four Roads to Mogadishu*, Simone Brioni (ed.), Alberto Carpi (trans.), Roma, Kimerafilm, 2012, p. 24.

140 Roberta Di Carmine, *Italophone Writing and The Intellectual Space of Creativity. Shirin Ramzanali Fazel and "Lontano da Mogadiscio"*, in "Quaderni del '900" 4 (2004), p. 49.

141 David Laitin, *Politics, Language, and Thought: The Somali Experience*, Chicago, University of Chicago Press, 1977, p. 163.

142 Serena Morassutti, *Intervista a Shirin Ramzanali Fazel*, in "Kuma" (2009), http://www.disp.let.uniroma1.it/kuma/poetica/kuma17morassutti.pdf [accessed 2 August 2013; my translation].

143 Shirin Ramzanali Fazel, *Lontano da Mogadiscio. Far From Mogadishu*, cit., p. 232. The devastation of the multicultural environment of Mogadishu due to the civil war is also remembered by Shirin in the short story *Mukulaal*. See Shirin Ramzanali Fazel, *Mukulaal (Cat)*, in *Roma d'Abissinia. Cronache dai resti dell'impero. Asmara, Mogadiscio, Addis Abeba*, Daniele Comberiati (ed.), Cuneo, Nerosubianco, 2010, pp. 13-22.

144 Nuruddin Farah, *Links*, New York, Riverhead, 2004, p. 227.

145 Ibid. pp. 226-227.

146 Lorenzo Mari, "'It was no mean feat for a housewife'. Shirin Ramzanali Fazel's *Lontano da Mogadiscio* (1994) in Nuruddin Farah's *Links* (2004)", 2012 [paper at the conference "Interrogating Cosmopolitan Conviviality. New Dimensions of the European in Literature', Otto-Friedrich-Universität Bamberg, 25 May].

147 Ibid.

148 Nuruddin Farah, cit., p. 252.

149 Lorenzo Mari, cit.

150 Alessandra Atti di Sarro, *Introduzione*, in Shirin Ramzanali Fazel, *Lontano da Mogadiscio*, Roma, Datanews, 1994, p. 9 [my translation].

151 Ibid., p. 10 [my translation].

152 Ibid. [my translation].

153 Shirin Ramzanali Fazel, *Lontano da Mogadiscio. Far From Mogadishu*, cit., p. 228.

154 Ibid.

155 Ibid., p. 242.

156 Ibid., p. 290.

157 Cinzia Sartini Blum, *Rewriting the Journey in Contemporary Italian Literature: Figures of Subjectivity in Progress*, Toronto, University of Toronto Press, 2008, p. 243.

158 Shirin compares the travel experience of a tourist and a migrant also in the story *Villaggio globale*. See Shirin Ramzanali Fazel, *Villaggio globale*, in "El ghibli. Rivista online di letteratura della migrazione" 30 (2010), http://www.el-ghibli.provincia.bologna.it/id_1-issue_07_30-section_1-index_pos_4.html [accessed 2 August 2013].

159 Luigi Marfè, *Italian Counter-Travel Writing: Images of Italy in Contemporary Migration Literature*, in "Studies in Travel Writing" 16.2 (2012), p. 192.

160 Ibid., p. 194.

161 Alessandra Atti di Sarro, cit., p. 8 [my translation].

162 Roberta Di Carmine, *Italophone Writing and The Intellectual Space of Creativity. Shirin Ramzanali Fazel and "Lontano da Mogadiscio"*, in "Quaderni del '900" 4 (2004), p.48.

163 Shirin Ramzanali Fazel, *Lontano da Mogadiscio. Far From Mogadishu*, cit., p. 276.

164 Graziella Parati, *Migration Italy. The Art of Talking Back in a Destination Culture*, Toronto, University of Toronto Press, 2005, p. 8.

165 Ibid., p. 65.

166 Ibid., p. 66.

167 Lucie Benchouiha, *"Dov'è la mia casa?". Questions of Home in Shirin Ramzanali Fazel's "Lontano da Mogadiscio"*, in "Quaderni del '900" 4 (2004), p. 41.

168 Shirin Ramzanali Fazel, *Lontano da Mogadiscio. Far From Mogadishu*, cit., p. 300.

169 Ibid., p. 300. It should be noted that the condition which Shirin very much resembles is that of the *meticcio* protagonist of *Clouds on the Equator*, considered to be "out of place" in Italy: "As a dark-skinned Italian, she did not feel at home at all". See Shirin Ramzanali Fazel, *Nuvole sull'equatore*, cit., p. 194.

170 Lucie Benchouiha, *"Dov'è la mia casa?"*, cit., p. 38.

171 Shirin Ramzanali Fazel, *Lontano da Mogadiscio. Far From Mogadishu*, cit., pp. 302.

172 Nathan Vetri, *Transgression, Integration, Suspension: The Sense Wars / Space Wars of the Body in Italian Literature and Film 2011*, in *The Cultures of Italian Migration*, Graziella Parati, Anthony Julian Tamburri (eds.), Madison, Farleigh Dickinson University Press, p. 174.

173 Lucie Benchouiha, *"Dov'è la mia casa?"*, cit., p. 36.

174 Jennifer Burns, *Migrant Imaginaries: Figures in Italian Migration Literature*, Oxford, Peter Lang, 2013, p. 126.

175 Ibid., p. 127.

176 Ibid., p. 122.

177 Alessandra Atti di Sarro, cit., p. 10 [my translation].

178 Ibid., p. 8 [my translation].

179 Ibid., pp. 8-9 [my translation].

180 On this topic, see Jennifer Burns, *Migrant Imaginaries*, cit., pp.16, 196.

181 Shirin Ramzanali Fazel, *Il segreto di Ommdurmann*, in "El-ghibli. Rivista online di letteratura della migrazione" 23 (2009), http://www.el-ghibli.provincia.bologna.it/index.php?id=2&issue=05_23&sezione=2&testo=2 [accessed 2 August 2013; this story was published for the first time in "Studi d'Italianistica nell'Africa Australe/ Italian Studies in Southern Africa" 8.2 (1995)].

182 Shirin Ramzanali Fazel, Gabriel, in "El-ghibli. Rivista online di letteratura della migrazione" 19 (2008), http://www.el-ghibli.provincia.bologna.it/id_1-issue_04_19-section_1-index_pos_3.html [accessed 2 August 2013].

183 Shirin Ramzanali Fazel, *La spiaggia*, in "Scritture Migranti" 1, 2007, pp. 9-14.

184 Shirin Ramzanali Fazel, *Villaggio Globale*, cit.

185 Shirin Ramzanali Fazel, *Mukulaal (Gatto)*, cit.

186 Shirin Ramzanali Fazel, DNA, in "El-ghibli. Rivista online di letteratura della migrazione" 33 (2011), http://www.el-ghibli.provincia.bologna.it/id_1-issue_08_33-section_1-index_pos_2.html [accessed 2 August 2013].

187 Simone Brioni, *Orientalism and Former Italian Colonies. An Interview with Shirin Ramzanali Fazel*, in *Orientalismi italiani Vol. 1*, Gabriele Proglio (ed.), Torino, Antares, 2012, p. 224.

188 Jennifer Burns and Shirin Ramzanali Fazel, *Narrating Mogadishu*, http://www2.warwick.ac.uk/fac/cross_fac/ias/current/earlycareer/events/migration/podcast/ [accessed 2 August 2013; conversation-interview held at the seminar 'Migration, Discrimination and Belonging: Transnational Spaces in Post-colonial Europe' at the University of Warwick, 6 March 2013].

189 Patrizia Ceola, *Migrazioni Narranti. L'Africa degli scrittori italiani e l'Italia degli scrittori africani: un chiasmo culturale e linguistico*, Padova, Libreria Universitaria, 2011, p. 245 [my translation].

190 Jennifer Burns, *Fragments of Impegno. Interpretations of Commitment in Contemporary Italian Narrative, 1980-2000*, Leeds, Northern University Press, 2001, p. 177.

191 Graziella Parati, *Migration Italy*, cit., pp.115-116.

192 Shirin Ramzanali Fazel, *Lontano da Mogadiscio. Far From Mogadishu*, cit., p. 274.

193 Jennifer Burns, *Migrant Imaginaries*, cit., p. 125.

194 Shirin Ramzanali Fazel, *Lontano da Mogadiscio. Far From Mogadishu*, cit., p. 307.

195 Raffaele Taddeo, *Lontano da Mogadiscio*, in "El ghibli. Rivista online di letteratura della migrazione" 23 (2009), http://www.el-ghibli.provincia.bologna.it/id_1-issue_06_24-section_6-index_pos_1.html [accessed 2 August 2013; my translation].

196 Loredana Polezzi, *Mixing Mother Tongues: Language, Narrative and the Spaces of Memory in Postcolonial Works by Italian Women Writers (Part 2)*, in "Romance Studies" 24.3 (2006), p. 219.

197 Rhiannon Noel Welch, *Intimate Truth and (Post)colonial Knowledge in Shirin Ramzanali Fazel's* Lontano da Mogadiscio, in *National Belongings: Hybridity in Italian Colonial and Postcolonial Cultures*, Jacqueline Andall, Derek Duncan (eds.), London, Peter Lang, 2010, p. 217.

198 Jennifer Burns, *Fragments of Impegno*, cit., p. 177.

199 Ibid., p. 162.

200 Shirin Ramzanali Fazel, *Lontano da Mogadiscio. Far From Mogadishu*, cit., p. 202.

201 Rebecca Hopkins, cit. [my translation].

202 Rhiannon Noel Welch, cit., p. 221.

203 Shirin Ramzanali Fazel, *Lontano da Mogadiscio. Far From Mogadishu*, cit., p. 202.

204 Ibid., p. 204.

205 Rebecca Hopkins, cit. [my translation].

206 Karen Blixen, *Out of Africa*, London, Penguin, 2001 (1937). According to Ngugi wa Thiong'o this text is as well-known as it is dangerous, since it does not only offer a fantastical and stereotyped image of Africa, but often compares the natives to animals, providing a powerful racist imaginary. See Ngugi wa Thiong'o, *Her Cook, Her Dog: Karen Blixen's Africa*, in Ngugi wa Thiong'o, *Moving the Centre: The Struggle for Cultural Freedom*, London, Heinemann, 1993, pp. 150-153.

207 Graziella Parati, *Introduction*, in *Mediterranean Crossroads. Migration Literature in Italy*, Graziella Parati (ed.), Madison, Fairleight Dickinson Press, 1999, p. 30.

208 Roberta Di Carmine, *Italophone Writing and The Intellectual Space of Creativity*, cit., p. 47.

209 Shirin Ramzanali Fazel, *Mukulaal (Gatto)*, cit.

210 Daniele Comberiati, *Quando le periferie diventano centro: le identità delle città postcoloniali*, in *Roma d'Abissinia. Cronache dai resti dell'Impero: Asmara, Mogadiscio, Addis Abeba*, Daniele Comberiati (ed.), Cuneo, Nerosubianco, p. 84 [my translation].

211 Alessandra Atti di Sarro, cit., p. 9 [my translation].

212 Raffaele Taddeo, cit. [my translation].

213 Rebecca Hopkins, cit. [my translation].

214 Raffaele Taddeo, cit. [my translation].

215 Jennifer Burns, *Fragments of Impegno*, p. 177.

216 Monica Venturini, *"Toccare il futuro". Scritture postcoloniali femminili*, in *Fuori centro. Percorsi postcoloniali nella letteratura italiana*, Roberto Derobertis (ed.), Roma, Aracne, 2010, p.123 [my translation].

217 Shirin Ramzanali Fazel, *Lontano da Mogadiscio. Far From Mogadishu*, cit., p. 234.

218 Gabriella Romani, *Italian Identity and Immigrant Writing: The Shaping of a New Discourse*, in *ItaliAfrica: Bridging Continents and Cultures*, Sante Matteo (ed.), Stony Brook, Forum Italicum, 2001, p. 371.

219 Lucie Benchouiha, *Hybrid Identities? Immigrant Women's Writing in Italy*, in "Italian Studies" 61.2, 2006, p. 255.

220 Shirin Ramzanali Fazel, *Le storie intrecciate della diaspora somala*, cit., p. 22.

221 Shirin Ramzanali Fazel, *Gezira*, in *Sandwell's Book of Happiness – Second Edition*, Birmingham, Sandwell NHS, 2012, p. 16, http://well-happy.co.uk/media/display/SPCT-HappinessBooklet-Jun12-web_frie.pdf [accessed 2 August 2013].

222 Loredana Polezzi, *Polylingual Writing in Today's Italy*, in *New Perspectives in Italian Cultural Studies Definition*, Vol. 1, Madison, Fairleigh Dickinson University Press, 2012.

223 Jennifer Burns, *Fragments of Impegno*, cit., p. 177.

Bibliography

Maria Abebù Viarengo, *Andiamo a spasso? Scirscir'n demna*, in "Linea d'ombra" 54 (1992), pp. 75-128.

Alessandra Atti di Sarro, *Introduzione*, in Shirin Ramzanali Fazel, *Lontano da Mogadiscio*, Roma, Datanews, 1994, pp. 7-10.

Lucie Benchouiha, *"Dov'è la mia casa?". Questions of Home* in Shirin Ramzanali Fazel's "Lontano da Mogadiscio", in "Quaderni del '900" 4 (2004), pp. 35-46

Lucie Benchouiha, *Hybrid Identities? Immigrant Women's Writing in Italy*, in "Italian Studies" 61.2, 2006, pp. 251-262.

Karen Blixen, *Out of Africa*, London, Penguin, 2001 (1937).

Simone Brioni, *Coincidenze*, in *Somalitalia. Quattro vie per Mogadiscio. Somalitalia. Four Roads to Mogadishu*, Simone Brioni (ed.), Roma, Kimerafilm, 2012 [special content of the documentary *Per un discorso postcoloniale italiano: parole chiave*].

————, *Orientalism and Former Italian Colonies. An Interview with Shirin Ramzanali Fazel'*, in *Orientalismi italiani*, Vol. 1, Gabriele Proglio (ed.), Torino, Antares, 2012, pp. 215-225.

Jennifer Burns, *Fragments of Impegno. Interpretations of Commitment in Contemporary Italian Narrative, 1980-2000*, Leeds, Northern University Press, 2001.

Jennifer Burns, *Frontiere nel testo: autori, collaborazioni e mediazioni nella scrittura italofona della migrazione*, in Jennifer Burns, Loredana Polezzi (eds.), *Borderlines: Migrazioni e identità nel Novecento*, Isernia, Cosmo Iannone, 2003, pp. 203-212.

————, *Migrant Imaginaries: Figures in Italian Migration Literature*, Oxford, Peter Lang, 2013.

————, *Outside Voices Within: Immigration Literature in Italian*, in *Trends in Contemporary Italian Narrative 1980-2007*, in Ania Gillian, Ann Hallamore Caesar (eds.), Cambridge, Cambridge Scholars, 2007, pp. 136-154.

———— and Shirin Ramzanali Fazel, *Narrating Mogadishu*, http://www2.warwick.ac.uk/fac/cross_fac/ias/current/earlycareer/events/migration/podcast/ [accessed 2 August 2013; conversation-interview held at the seminar 'Migration, Discrimination and Belonging: Transnational Spaces in Post-colonial Europe' at the University of Warwick, 6 March 2013].

Patrizia Ceola, *Migrazioni Narranti. L'Africa degli scrittori italiani e l'Italia degli scrittori africani: un chiasmo culturale e linguistico*, Padova, Libreria Universitaria, 2011.

Daniele Comberiati, *Quando le periferie diventano centro: le identità delle città postcoloniali*, in *Roma d'Abissinia. Cronache dai resti dell'Impero: Asmara, Mogadiscio, Addis Abeba*, Daniele Comberiati (ed.), Cuneo, Nerosubianco, 2010, pp.75-95.

Lidia Curti, *Voices of a Minor Empire: Migrant Women Writers in Contemporary Italy*, in *The Cultures of Italian Migration*, Graziella Parati, Anthony Julian Tamburri (eds.), Madison, Fairleigh Dickinson University Press, 2011, pp.45-58.

Angelo Del Boca, *Una sconfitta dell'intelligenza. Italia e Somalia*, Roma-Bari, Laterza, 1993.

———, *I crimini del colonialismo fascista*, in *Le guerre coloniali del fascismo*, Angelo Del Boca (ed.), Roma-Bari, Laterza, 1991, pp. 232-255.

Roberta Di Carmine, *Italophone Writing and The Intellectual Space of Creativity. Shirin Ramzanali Fazel and "Lontano da Mogadiscio"*, in "Quaderni del '900" 4 (2004), pp. 47-54.

Rebecca Hopkins, *Somalia: passato, presente e futuro. Intervista con la scrittrice Shirin Ramzanali Fazel*, in "El-ghibli. Rivista online di letteratura della migrazione" 18 (2007), http://www.el-ghibli.provincia.bologna.it/id_1-issue_04_18-section_6-index_pos_1.html [accessed 2 August 2013].

I campi fascisti: Dalle guerre in Africa alla Repubblica di Salò, www.campifascisti.it [accessed 2 August 2013].

David Laitin, *Politics, Language, and Thought: The Somali Experience*, Chicago, University of Chicago Press, 1977.

Luigi Marfè, *Italian Counter-Travel Writing: Images of Italy in Contemporary Migration Literature*, in "Studies in Travel Writing" 16.2 (2012), pp. 191-201.

Lorenzo Mari, *"'It was no mean feat for a housewife'. Shirin Ramzanali Fazel's Lontano da Mogadiscio (1994) in Nuruddin Farah's Links (2004)"*, 2012 [paper at the conference "Interrogating Cosmopolitan Conviviality. New Dimensions of the European in Literature', Otto-FriedrichUniversität Bamberg, 25 May].

Luigi Meneghello, *Materia di Reading e altri reperti*, Milano, Rizzoli, 2005.

Serena Morassutti, *Intervista a Shirin Ramzanali Fazel*, in "*Kuma*" (2009), http://www.disp.let.uniroma1.it/kuma/poetica/kuma17morassutti.pdf [accessed 2 August 2013].

Antonio Maria Morone, *L'ultima colonia: Come l'Italia è ritornata in Somalia 1950- 1960*, Bari-Roma, Laterza, 2011.

Ngugi wa Thiong'o, *Her Cook, Her Dog: Karen Blixen's Africa*, in Ngugi wa Thiong'o, *Moving the Centre: The Struggle for Cultural Freedom*, London, Heinemann, 1993, pp. 150-153.

Nuruddin Farah, *Links*, New York, Riverhead, 2004. Graziella Parati, *Migration Italy. The Art of Talking Back in a Destination Culture*, Toronto, University of Toronto Press, 2005.

―――, *Introduction*, in *Mediterranean Crossroads. Migration Literature in Italy*, Graziella Parati (ed.), Madison, Fairleight Dickinson Press, 1999, pp. 13-42.

Roberta Pergher, *Impero immaginato, impero vissuto. Recenti sviluppi nella storiografia del colonialismo italiano*, in "Ricerche di Storia Politica" 1 (2007), pp. 53-66.

Loredana Polezzi, *Mixing Mother Tongues: Language, Narrative and the Spaces of Memory in Postcolonial Works by Italian Women Writers (Part 2)*, in "Romance Studies" 24.3 (2006), pp. 215-225.

―――, *Polylingual Writing in Today's Italy*, in *New Perspectives in Italian Cultural Studies Definition, Vol. 1*, Madison, Fairleigh Dickinson University Press, 2012.

Ribka Sibhatu, *Aulò. Canto poesia dell'Eritrea*, Roma, Sinnos, 1993.

Gabriella Romani, *Italian Identity and Immigrant Writing: The Shaping of a New Discourse*, in *ItaliAfrica: Bridging Continents and Cultures*, Sante Matteo (ed.), Stony Brook, Forum Italicum, 2001, pp. 363-375.

Cinzia Sartini Blum, *Rewriting the Journey in Contemporary Italian Literature: Figures of Subjectivity in Progress*, Toronto, University of Toronto Press, 2008.

Roberto Scardova (ed.), *Carte false: l'assassinio di Ilaria Alpi e Miran Hrovatin. Quindici anni senza verità*, Roma, Ambiente, 2009.

Igiaba Scego, *Shirin Ramzanali F. Scrittrice Nomade*, in "Internazionale" 732 (22 February 2008), pp. 60-62.

Shirin Ramzanali Fazel, DNA, in "El-ghibli. Rivista online di letteratura della migrazione" 33 (2011), http://www.el-ghibli.provincia.bologna.it/id_1-issue_08_33-section_1-index_pos_2.html [accessed 2 August 2013].

———, *Gabriel*, in "El-ghibli. Rivista online di letteratura della migrazione" 19 (2008), http://www.el-ghibli.provincia.bologna.it/id_1-issue_04_19-section_1-index_pos_3.html [accessed 2 August 2013].

———, *Gezira*, in *Sandwell's Book of Happiness – Second Edition*, Birmingham, Sandwell NHS, 2012, p. 16, http://well-happy.co.uk/media/display/SPCT-HappinessBooklet-Jun12-web_frie.pdf [accessed 2 August 2013].

———, *Il segreto di Ommdurmann*, in "El-ghibli. Rivista online di letteratura della migrazione" 23 (2009), http://www.el-ghibli.provincia.bologna.it/index.php?id=2&issue=05_23&sezione=2&testo=2 [accessed 2 August 2013; the story was published for the first time in "Studi d'Italianistica nell'Africa Australe/Italian Studies in Southern Africa" 8.2 (1995)].

———, *Lontano da Mogadiscio*, Roma, Datanews, 1994.

———, *Lontano da Mogadiscio. Far From Mogadishu*, Simone Bioni (ed.), Milano, Laurana, 2013.

———, *La spiaggia*, in "Scritture Migranti" 1, 2007, pp. 9-14.

———, *Le storie intrecciate della diaspora somala. The Intervowen Stories of Somali Diaspora*, in *Somalitalia: Quattro Vie per Mogadiscio. Somalitalia: Four Roads to Mogadishu*, Simone

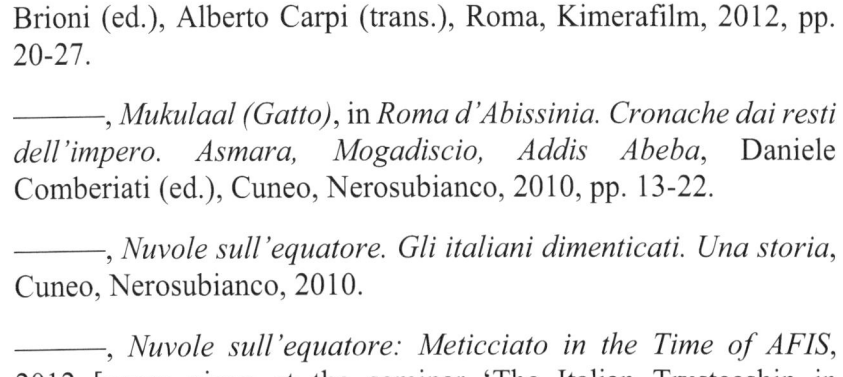

Brioni (ed.), Alberto Carpi (trans.), Roma, Kimerafilm, 2012, pp. 20-27.

———, *Mukulaal (Gatto)*, in *Roma d'Abissinia. Cronache dai resti dell'impero. Asmara, Mogadiscio, Addis Abeba*, Daniele Comberiati (ed.), Cuneo, Nerosubianco, 2010, pp. 13-22.

———, *Nuvole sull'equatore. Gli italiani dimenticati. Una storia*, Cuneo, Nerosubianco, 2010.

———, *Nuvole sull'equatore: Meticciato in the Time of AFIS*, 2012 [paper given at the seminar 'The Italian Trusteeship in Somalia (1950-1960) and Beyond' at the University of Warwick, 18 January].

———, *Villaggio globale*, in "El ghibli. Rivista online di letteratura della migrazione" 30 (2010), http://www.el-ghibli.provincia.bologna.it/id_1-issue_07_30-section_1-index_pos_4.html [accessed 2 August 2013].

Raffaele Taddeo, *Lontano da Mogadiscio*, in "El ghibli. Rivista online di letteratura della migrazione" 23 (2009), http://www.el-ghibli.provincia.bologna.it/id_1-issue_06_24-section_6-index_pos_1.html [accessed 2 August 2013].

Paolo Tripodi, *The Colonial Legacy in Somalia: Rome and Mogadishu: from Colonial Administration to Operation Restore Hope*, London, Palgrave-Mcmillan, 1999.

Monica Venturini *CONTROCÀNONe. Per una cartografia della scrittura coloniale e postcoloniale italiana*, Roma, Aracne, 2010.

———, *"Toccare il futuro". Scritture postcoloniali femminili*, in *Fuori centro. Percorsi postcoloniali nella letteratura italiana*, Roberto Derobertis (ed.), Roma, Aracne, 2010, pp.111-129.

Nathan Vetri, *Transgression, Integration, Suspension: The Sense Wars / Space Wars of the Body in Italian Literature and Film 2011*, in *The Cultures of Italian Migration*, Graziella Parati, Anthony Julian Tamburri (eds.), Madison, Farleigh Dickinson University Press, pp.169-184.

Rhiannon Noel Welch, *Intimate Truth and (Post)colonial Knowledge in Shirin Ramzanali Fazel's* Lontano da Mogadiscio, in *National Belongings: Hybridity in Italian Colonial and Postcolonial Cultures*, Jacqueline Andall, Derek Duncan (eds.), London, Peter Lang, 2010, pp. 215-234.

Sharon Wood, *A «Quattro Mani»: Collaboration in Italian Immigrant Literature*, in Sara Bigliazzi, Sharon Wood (eds.), *Collaboration in the Arts from the Middle Ages to the Present*, Ashgate, Aldershot, 2006, pp. 151-162.

Wu Ming, *Primavera Migrante*, in "Internazionale" (4 April 2013), http://www.internazionale.it/opinioni/wuming/2013/04/04/primavera-migrante/ [accessed 2 August 2013].

Wu Ming 1 and Roberto Santachiara, *Point Lenana*, Torino, Einaudi, 2013.

Wu Ming 2 and Antar Mohamed, *Timira. Romanzo Meticcio*, Torino, Einaudi, 2012.

My Thanks

Above all, I thank Allah (SWT); every praise is for Him, The Most Kind and The Most Merciful.

My gratitude and my approval go to those aid agencies and to those individuals who made a significant effort and sacrificed themselves to be close to a suffering population. Numberless are the gestures of great friendship and solidarity carried out by common people for my country during these dark and painful years.

I am grateful for the confidence that the Somalis of the Diaspora accorded me, entrusting me with their painful testimonies, making me part of the drama they experienced.

A sincere thank you goes to Simone Brioni, for the enthusiasm shown for this project and for his genuine interest towards Somalia.

I also thank Sandra Clyne, Claudia Panti and Kate Willman for the careful reading and revision of the drafts of the text.

Finally, heartfelt thanks to my dear friend Barbara Neave, for the encouragement and for her sincere appreciation of my work.

I thank David Rollason for his work on the design and final layout for this current production of my work.

Printed in Great Britain
by Amazon